Alice Louise James

Catering for Two

Comfort and Economy for Small Households

Alice Louise James

Catering for Two
Comfort and Economy for Small Households

ISBN/EAN: 9783744643542

Printed in Europe, USA, Canada, Australia, Japan

Cover: Foto ©Suzi / pixelio.de

More available books at **www.hansebooks.com**

CATERING FOR TWO

COMFORT AND ECONOMY
FOR SMALL HOUSEHOLDS

BY

ALICE L. JAMES

SECOND IMPRESSION

G. P. PUTNAM'S SONS
NEW YORK AND LONDON
The Knickerbocker Press
1899

PREFACE.

THE difficulty of reducing the average rules of the cook books to meet the wants of a family of two or three, added to the urgent solicitations of friends, has suggested to the writer the need of this little book.

Dining well on small means is an art only to be acquired by long experience, and the object of the following chapters is to give the result of sixteen years' labor and study, so that the way may be made easier for others just taking upon themselves the duties of a housewife.

In the accompanying menus the directions are exact and absolutely reliable.

There is no indefinite "a little" of this, or "just enough" of that, to puzzle the beginner, and the dishes, which are nourishing and appetizing, are inexpensive as well, a consideration not always taken into account.

Catering for Two is for the inexperienced cook, and while the proportions are limited to the needs of two, or at most three, it is only necessary to double the rules to make the quantities sufficient for the ordinary family.

CONTENTS.

	PAGE
DINNERS	1
COMPANY LUNCHEONS	183
BREAKFAST, TEA, AND LUNCHEON DISHES.	192
FANCY DESSERTS	229
MISCELLANEOUS RECIPES	245
HELPFUL SUGGESTIONS . . .	262
INDEX	281

CATERING FOR TWO.

DINNERS.

I.

Consommé with rice.
Oyster pie.
Pickled cabbage.   Grape jelly.
Egg salad with greens.
Crackers.   Cheese.
Roly-poly peach pudding.
Egg sauce.
Tea or coffee.   Caramel jelly.

Alternative: Round steak (fried).
Farina pudding.

CONSOMMÉ WITH RICE.

Get a shank of mutton weighing about two pounds, or two shanks weighing a pound each. Wipe with a damp cloth and cut off any dried outer skin, dredge with two tablespoonfuls of flour, pour on a quart of cold water, and, after soaking a few hours, simmer for several hours, covered closely.

Strain off this liquor, pour over the bones and meat enough cold water to cover, and cook again for another hour. Strain and add to the first quantity of liquor and throw away the bones and meat. Salt to taste, add an onion, carrot, and turnip, and cook until the vegetables are tender ; these may be put away for a salad, and when the broth is cold, take off the cake of fat. There should be nearly a quart of solid jelly. Take a pint of this, add a tablespoonful of washed rice, and cook gently until the rice is tender.

A little minced parsley may be added at the last moment.

This broth is much relished by the sick, and may be varied in many ways.

OYSTER PIE.

Twenty-five medium-sized freshened oysters.

Slice very thin a cupful of raw potatoes, pour on them one cup of rich, sweet milk, cover the dish (of earthenware) closely, and cook on top of the stove until done. Do not stir them, but watch carefully that they do not burn.

When the potatoes are cool, place the oysters on top of them, pepper and salt lightly, add the oyster liquor and a tablespoonful of butter in small pieces. Place over all a cover of pie-crust, made as follows, and bake in a very hot oven for fifteen minutes.

Sift together a cup of flour and half a teaspoonful of salt and cut into it with a knife two heaping tablespoonfuls of lard as cold and hard as ice can make it.

When the lard is the size of peas, stir in with a fork four tablespoonfuls of ice-water, and mould quickly into a ball; flour the moulding-board, roll out once, cut a few little slits or fancy figures in the centre, and lay upon the oysters. Trim off the overlapping edges and bake at once. Make any paste that is left into a little tart.

ROLY-POLY PUDDING (BAKED).

Sift together one cup of flour, one teaspoonful of baking powder, and half a teaspoonful of salt. Chop this with a scant half-cup of suet (ice cold) and mix quickly with two thirds of a cup of ice-cold water.

Mould into a long roll and roll out on a floured moulding-board as thin as it will hold together.

Have ready three or four peeled and sliced fine juicy peaches (canned will do), cover the paste with them, dredge lightly with flour, and roll up like a jelly roll.

Place in an earthen dish, and bake in a moderately hot oven for three quarters of an hour.

Serve hot with the following sauce:

Cream with a fork a half-cup of sweet butter, add a cupful of granulated sugar, and stir well; then add the yolk of a small egg and stir, then the frothed white, whipping the whole until very light.

Now add a quarter-cupful of boiling water, set over the teakettle, and cook and stir for several minutes. It should be a little thick, and quite foamy.

Flavor with a tablespoonful of wine or brandy, or vanilla to taste.

This sauce will keep a week or longer in a cool place, and may be warmed up by setting over a teakettle.

The pudding may be warmed in the oven in a covered dish.

PICKLED CABBAGE.

One cabbage, solid and crisp.

Two ounces mustard seed, one heaping tablespoonful of black pepper.

Two tablespoonfuls of salt, one quart cider vinegar, three onions, one red-pepper pod, one tablespoonful sugar, one heaping tablespoonful mixed spices, whole cloves, cinnamon, allspice, and a speck of mace. Tie the spices in a piece of cheese-cloth, giving them plenty of room.

Chop the cabbage, or, if preferred, shave into ribbons, put it with the onions and pepper pod chopped fine into an earthen crock, in alternate layers with the salt, pepper, and mustard seed.

Stamp with a potato masher, to press all together closely, but not hard enough to bruise the cabbage. Put the bag of spices on top, and over the whole lay a heavy plate, pouring the vinegar on at the last. Put on the cover of the jar and set in a cool place. It will be ready for the table in a few days, and will keep for months in cool weather if made after frost sets in.

The vinegar must not be heated, nor the cabbage. Everything is in the raw state for this pickle.

CARAMEL JELLY.

Melt one heaping tablespoonful of gelatine in two tablespoonfuls of cold water, add the juice and grated rind of half a lemon, three tablespoonfuls of granulated sugar, a pinch of ground cinnamon, a teaspoonful of sugar burned brown, a few grains of salt, and one cupful and four tablespoonfuls of boiling water (in hot weather omit the extra four tablespoons of boiling water). Stir and strain, and set away to harden on ice.

This makes a delicious dessert with whipped cream (and gelatine) heaped on top.

FRIED ROUND STEAK.

Ask for the prime cut of round steak.

Trim off the outer edges of fat, cut a piece from the steak large enough for a meal, and pound with a hammer until it becomes like jelly. Press into shape and fry in a smoking-hot spider; it will take only a minute for each side to become brown, as the fire must be very hot.

Place upon a bed of fresh water-cresses. Add a tablespoonful of butter to the spider, which must now be slightly cooled, stir in an even teaspoonful of flour, salt, and pepper; pour in four tablespoonfuls of boiling water, cook a minute, and pour over the steak. Serve at once. The remainder of the steak may be broiled or made into a beefsteak pudding with suet crust.

FARINA PUDDING.

Stir with a spoon a cup and a half of boiling milk until it whirls, then slowly pour in a heaping tablespoonful of farina, stirring all the time. Add one fourth of an even teaspoonful of salt, cook five minutes, and then set in another saucepan containing boiling water and cook, covered, fifteen minutes, stirring occasionally. Flavor with lemon or vanilla and turn into cups.

Serve cold with sweetened cream.

II.

Chicken broth.
Sirloin steak (oven roast).
Lyonnaise potatoes.
Macaroni with cheese.
Stewed peaches or prunes.
Tomato salad.   French dressing.
Whipped-cream cake.
Stewed strawberries.   Tea or coffee.

Alternative : Beef stew with sweet potatoes.
Tomato fritters.

CHICKEN BROTH.

Put into a kettle the neck, lower parts of the leg, and the wing tips of a large fat fowl.

Dredge with flour and add a pint of cold water. After soaking an hour, simmer gently, closely covered, until the meat drops from the bones, strain and put the broth back on the fire, then add a cupful more water to the bones and cook an hour longer; add this liquor also to the broth and throw away the chicken.

There should be a scant pint of broth.

Season with onion juice, salt and pepper, and a little parsley, boil up, and serve with squares of bread toasted brown in the oven.

Make chicken salad of the body of the fowl.

SIRLOIN STEAK.

A prime cut of sirloin steak will weigh about two pounds and a half. Cut off enough for two broils, and use the rest for the oven roast. Trim off the outside edges of fat, dust the meat lightly with pepper and flour, and roll it into a compact roll, pinning securely together with a long clinch-nail.

These nails may be found at a hardware store, and are just the thing to use for little roasts. Broil the meat over a clear, fierce bed of coals just long enough to seal up the juices (hastening the process as much as possible).

Place a piece of fat on a baking-tin, put the meat upon it, and roast in a hot oven for about twenty minutes. Take from the oven, remove the skewers, being careful not to disturb the shape of the meat, sprinkle with salt, and pour over a gravy made by adding a scant half-cupful of boiling water to the baking-pan in which a teaspoonful of flour has been browned; salt to taste and pour off the grease.

LYONNAISE POTATOES.

Slice a cupful of onions and two cupfuls of cold boiled or baked potatoes.

Put them in alternate layers in a baking-dish for the table. Cream a tablespoonful of butter with a teaspoonful of flour, add half a teaspoonful of salt and a cupful of boiling milk, cook up, and pour over the potatoes and onions.

Dust with pepper and bake half an hour, uncovered, in a moderate oven, or cover and cook on top of the stove; they are better baked, however.

MACARONI WITH CHEESE.

Soak half a cupful of macaroni in two cups of boiling water twenty minutes, then boil until tender,—about thirty minutes.

Skim out the macaroni, put into an earthen dish, sprinkle with half a teaspoonful of salt, a dust of pepper, and spread over the top thin slices of old English cheese.

Add a teaspoonful of butter and half a cup of milk.

Bake twenty minutes and serve in the baking-dish.

TOMATO SALAD.

Serve the tomatoes (pared) on lettuce leaves, either with a mayonnaise or French dressing. They must be ice cold, to be good.

WHIPPED-CREAM CAKE.

Sift three times one and a half cupfuls of flour lightly put into the measure, with one and a half teaspoonfuls of baking-powder, and one scant half-teaspoonful of salt.

Rub into the flour a lump of butter the size of an egg (this will be a little less than a fourth of a cupful).

Put an egg into a bowl, pour on one scant cupful of sugar, and beat together, then add slowly two thirds of a cupful of water. Add flavoring, and pour slowly into the flour, beating it in with the hand until the batter is smooth and foamy.

This should take about five minutes; the hand should be freshly washed in hot water for the purpose, and the fingers must be spread apart in order to beat properly.

Fill two shallow layer-cake pans half full, not more, and bake in a hot oven. When cold, put between and on the top layer two thirds of a cup of cream whipped to a stiff froth. Keep in a cold place several hours before serving.

The remainder of the batter may be made into little drop cakes, half a teaspoonful for each, and baked on the bottom of inverted tins.

If whipped cream is not at hand, proceed as follows, making a lemon cake.

LEMON CAKE.

Dissolve half a teaspoonful of corn-starch in one tablespoonful of cold water, add three tablespoonfuls of boiling water, a few grains of salt, and boil several minutes. Put into a deep bowl two cupfuls of confectioner's sugar, and one third of the juice of one lemon. Add by the teaspoonful enough of the corn-starch mixture to make a paste thin enough to spread easily between and on top of the cakes. This is a delicious frosting for any cake, and it will always be soft. Orange may be substituted for lemon if preferred.

STEWED STRAWBERRIES.

One cupful of water, one cupful of sugar, three cupfuls berries, measured after being picked over and rinsed. Boil the sugar and water until clear, add the berries, and cook two or three minutes after boiling begins. This rule will serve for blackberries and raspberries also, and may be used when canning these fruits. Fruit should always be put into a boiling syrup; and this is the rule for dried fruits also. They should never be soaked; simply washed, and put immediately into the boiling syrup. A cupful of berries with a third of a cup each of sugar and water is enough for one meal.

STEWED PEACHES (RIPE).

Rub the down from the peaches with a coarse towel, quarter and stone them.

Allow one tablespoonful of sugar and one tablespoonful of water for every medium-sized peach.

Put the stones, water, and sugar on to boil for a few minutes, remove the former, put in the fruit, and when boiling begins cook gently for five minutes.

Peaches may be peeled if liked, but the skins are very delicious.

They may be baked by cutting in halves, filling with a tablespoonful of sugar, and adding a tablespoonful of water to the pan.

Cover and bake.

STEWED PRUNES (RICH).

Make a syrup of two cups of water and one cup of sugar, add half a lemon thinly sliced, and one pound of prunes which have been rinsed, but not soaked, in cold water. Simmer gently in a covered earthen or agate-ware vessel for four hours. Then pour over them a syrup made of one cupful of sugar and one (or two) cupfuls of boiling water cooked together ten minutes.

Boil the prunes a few minutes longer and serve either hot or cold.

Covered, in a cool place they will keep weeks.

The little Turkish prune is the best, and this will not need the lemon.

BEEF STEW WITH SWEET POTATOES.

Have one pound of chuck or stewing beef cut into two-inch pieces.

Dredge with a tablespoon of flour, add a tablespoonful of fried salt pork cut into dice (but not the grease), and either a piece of red-pepper pod the size of a thumb-nail, or a pinch of cayenne.

Use an earthen or agate vessel with a fitted cover, and simmer the meat for two hours in a scant cupful of boiling water. Then add two small sweet potatoes, peeled and washed; add a scant teaspoonful of salt, cook until the potatoes are done, and serve on a platter.

Be careful not to break the potatoes.

III.

Broth.

Mutton with caper sauce.
Boiled rice.
Parsnip with cream sauce.
Crab-apple jelly.   Bread and butter.
Celery hearts.   Neufchatel cheese.
Salted Saratoga chip crackers.
Steamed dumpling (raised).
Caramel sauce.
Canned or stewed fresh cherries, strawberries, or peaches.
Oranges.   Tea or coffee.

BROTH.

Take the bone cut from a mutton shank weighing a pound and a half.

Cover with a quart of cold water, and, after soaking an hour or so, heat gradually, and boil gently until meat and bone separate.

This will take several hours. Then add two tablespoonfuls of tomatoes, one teaspoonful washed rice, half an onion, grated, and boil until there is a pint of broth. Strain, skim off fat, add salt to taste, and serve. A tiny pinch of red pepper is an addition.

BOILED MUTTON WITH CAPER SAUCE.

Get a shank of mutton weighing one and a half pounds. Trim off the outer skin, which generally is the cause of the "woolly taste" so often complained of in mutton.

Cut out the bone, dredge the meat on all sides with flour, dust with black pepper, and put it into a small deep agate pot with a close-fitting cover; pour over one and a half cupfuls of boiling water, and when boiling begins, set on the back of the stove to cook gently for about two hours.

When done, put the mutton on a deep platter and season with salt and pepper. Skim the fat from the gravy, which will be reduced to a cupful, add a teaspoonful of flour blended with a teaspoonful of butter, stir well, cook a few minutes, add salt to taste and one or two tablespoonfuls of capers, boil up, and serve either poured around the mutton or in a gravy tureen.

If capers are not liked, a spoonful of tomato catsup, or an onion sliced and cooked with the mutton, can be substituted. If greater delicacy is preferred, do not use the gravy at all, but make a white sauce, called drawn butter.

Mix an even tablespoonful of flour with a lump of butter the size of an egg, stir to a cream, and slowly add a cupful of boiling water, stirring and cooking several minutes. Add salt and pepper to taste, with the capers, boil up, and serve. A tablespoonful of minced parsley may be used instead of the capers. The gravy may be added to the broth, or it may form the basis of a soup for another day.

It is not safe to keep mutton stock more than twenty-four hours, except in freezing weather.

BOILED RICE.

Wash half a cupful of rice, drain, and pour it gradually into a pint of fast-boiling water, to which half an even teaspoonful of salt has been added. Stir all the time the rice is being poured in. Boil hard for a minute, then cover closely, and set upon a part of the stove where it will simmer for an hour or a little longer, covered all the time. The rice will be perfectly soft and yet retain its shape, and the water will all have been absorbed.

Heap on a dish, butter liberally, and dust with pepper.

PARSNIP WITH CREAM SAUCE.

Scrape and wash, but do not soak, a fine large parsnip. Cover it with boiling water and cook until tender.

Cut into slices half an inch thick, put into a vegetable dish, and pour over a sauce made by stirring to a cream one tablespoonful of butter and one of flour, and adding a cupful of boiling water, with salt and pepper to taste. This sauce should boil ten minutes.

Sometimes parsnips have a core so hard that no amount of boiling will make it tender.

From twenty to thirty minutes is the time allowed, and if the core still remains unyielding, cut it out of each slice and discard.

Any parsnip left over may be mashed and served in a little cake browned in a frying-pan.

CELERY HEARTS.

Wash the hearts of fine crisp celery, place upon a celery dish, and pass with Neufchatel cheese and Saratoga chip crackers, salted. It is not necessary to bring on fresh plates for this little course, as the bread-and-butter plates at each place will answer, if one wishes to save steps or time.

STEAMED DUMPLING.

One half yeast-cake, three quarters cup of water, or milk and water mixed, one heaping cup of flour, one half-teaspoonful of salt, one tablespoonful of sugar, one egg, heaping tablespoonful butter.

Melt the butter and yeast-cake in the warmed milk, beat the egg, and sift flour, salt, and sugar together.

Mix all these ingredients, and set in a warm place for one hour.

At the end of this time, beat the mixture, fill a mould one third full, and let the dough rise until it is nearly doubled in bulk, which will be in about half an hour. Set in a steamer and cook one hour, then cover and keep hot until ready to serve.

CARAMEL SAUCE FOR STEAMED DUMPLING.

Stir to a cream one tablespoonful of butter, two tablespoonfuls of confectioner's sugar. Add a little caramel (directions to follow) and the yolk of an egg. Beat for several minutes.

Add more, or all, of the caramel, and more sugar if desired, and, at the last, one tablespoonful of wine or brandy.

This pudding will keep a week in a cool place, if covered, and may be warmed for another meal by setting on a plate, covered closely with a bowl, and set in the oven, or in a steamer.

CARAMEL OR BURNT SUGAR.

To make the caramel, put on a cool part of the stove, to melt, four heaping tablespoonfuls of granulated sugar with two tablespoonfuls water, and let it cook gently for half an hour, covered. At this time it should be bright, coffee-brown syrup, clear as amber.

Be careful not to have the fire too hot, or the caramel will be burned and have a bitter taste. It must not be stirred, as this will grain the sugar, but the saucepan can be shifted from side to side, carefully, if necessary.

Now add to the syrup six tablespoonfuls boiling water, one spoonful at a time, pouring it directly into the middle of the mass. Let this boil gently for two minutes without stirring, then mix with a spoon, cooking and stirring for another minute.

There should be just a half-cupful of syrup, perfectly clear and free from lumps.

Cool before using.

ORANGES.

Select fine, large oranges. Soften them a little by rolling gently on the kitchen table with the hand.

Cut off an inch-thick slice from the stem end and replace it, so that the fruit will present a whole appearance.

Serve on dessert plates with orange spoons or stout teaspoons.

The choice or delicate teaspoons are apt to be twisted and ruined when used as orange scoops. The oranges may be cut in halves if preferred.

IV.

Tomato bisque.

Porter-house roast.
White turnips and potatoes mashed together.
Baked rhubarb sauce.

Celery salad.   Cream cheese.
Graham wafers.

Corn-starch pudding with candied fruits.

Tea or coffee.

Bread and butter served with second course.

TOMATO BISQUE.

Put the bone cut from a porter-house roast into an agate pot having a fitted cover, and soak for an hour or so in a quart of cold water. Then bring slowly to a boil and cook gently until the liquor is reduced to a cupful. Bone and meat should have dropped apart by this time (about four hours). Add half a cupful of tomatoes, in which is well mixed a dessert-spoonful of flour; add also a teaspoonful of onion juice, and boil gently for half an hour.

Strain, skim off the fat, return to the pot, and add half a cupful of milk (fresh and rich) in which a pinch of baking-soda has been dissolved. Stir well while heating, and when it boils up, season to taste and serve.

ROAST BEEF.

Order about three pounds from prime cut of porter-house roast. Have the bone taken out and sent home for soup-stock, and have also the long coarse end cut off and corned for twenty-four or thirty hours, or a little longer if preferred.

Cut off the outer edge of fat, as it is dry and likely to be bitter. Skewer the meat firmly with a long clinch-nail. These nails make the best skewers for small roasts or cuts, as, having broad, flat heads, they can be removed with ease.

The meat should now be browned on all sides. This is not necessary for large roasts, but for small ones; it is the best way to make them retain their juices and sweetness. Either broil over a fierce bed of coals, or fry in a smoking-hot frying-pan. The meat does not want to be cooked, only browned well, and this process should take but a few minutes. Now dredge with flour on all sides, pepper lightly, and place, fat side down, on a meat-rack (a wire tea-stand will do) in a small dripping-pan.

Roast in a hot oven for fifteen minutes, then add a half-cupful of boiling water, cover the meat with a pan, and in thirty minutes take from the oven.

Cut a deep, narrow slit, and pry apart to see if it is done to suit. If too rare return to the oven for fifteen or twenty minutes longer.

Never allow the water in the pan to boil entirely away, or the gravy will be scorched to bitterness; it should be merely browned.

Put the roast on a platter, dust on all sides with salt, and garnish with celery tops. Stir together a teaspoonful of flour, and enough cold water to blend together smoothly (about two tablespoonfuls), add this to the sediment in the dripping-pan, and boil up.

Add also a little boiling water and salt to taste. There should be half a cupful of gravy. Serve in a tureen. If the gravy is too pale, add a few drops of caramel.

If there is no sediment and no grease, which often occurs, put a tablespoonful of butter in the pan, brown it slightly, and then add flour and water as directed.

The meat is far more delicious when it keeps its juices while cooking.

In carving, cut across the grain, and always add to each plate a spoonful of red juice from the platter; this is called "dish gravy," and is the life of the meat.

The roast may be served for another dinner by

putting it in a moderate oven and simply heating it through.

For still another time, cut the meat into dice, always cutting across the grain, dredge with flour, and cover with boiling water.

Cover closely and stew gently from two to two and a half hours.

Add onions or tomatoes, or serve plain.

Salt and pepper to taste. Chop fine any which may be left, and add one fourth as much cold baked potatoes, a few drops of onion juice, a little flour, butter, and milk, and you have a hash for breakfast.

Either fry in cakes, or serve with dipped toast. When cutting meat for a stew do not use the fat; if you want fat, get salt pork and brown it, and use this without the grease.

If any hash is left, do not throw it away; it can go into the soup-pot with other scraps of meat, bones, and vegetables.

When the coarse end comes, which you have left with the butcher to be corned, cover it with a quart of boiling water, and cook gently for three hours. This piece is not good when hot; let it get cold in the liquor it boiled in, and slice for luncheon or tea, or make into hash.

Soups and corned beef may be cooked in a slow oven after they are started to boil on top of the stove, thus saving the house from the long-continued odors; onions and cabbage may be treated in the same way.

WHITE TURNIPS AND POTATOES MASHED TOGETHER.

Wash and peel two medium-sized potatoes and two turnips equal in size to the potatoes.

Cut in halves and cook, in enough boiling water to cover, from twenty minutes to half an hour. Test with a fork, and when tender drain by turning into a sieve or colander.

Return them to the pot which has been dried, mash thoroughly, add a dessert-spoonful of butter, and one third of a teaspoonful of salt. Stir with a fork and add more salt if needed. Heap in a vegetable tureen, smooth the top, put on a lump of butter the size of a walnut, sprinkle with pepper, and keep hot, uncovered in the oven, until wanted. If any is left, either make it into a little cake and fry in butter, or add to the soup vegetables.

CELERY SALAD.

Break into half-inch pieces one cupful of crisp, blanched celery stalks. Little tough strings will hold the pieces together; strip these off.

Make a dressing of one tablespoonful of olive-oil, a dash of cayenne pepper, one fourth of a teaspoonful of salt, and a teaspoonful of real cider vinegar.

Toss the celery about in this and serve in

shallow salad bowl, either on a bed of lettuce leaves, or garnished with watercress or parsley.

Pass Graham wafers and any preferred cream cheese, Eagle, or Philadelphia, Neufchatel, etc.

CORN-STARCH PUDDING WITH CANDIED FRUIT.

Put one cup of milk on the stove, and when it boils add two level tablespoonfuls of corn-starch mixed with a pinch of salt, and two tablespoonfuls cold milk. Boil for a few minutes, stirring constantly from the bottom and sides; then put the saucepan into another containing boiling water, cover, and stir occasionally to prevent a crust forming. Cook ten minutes.

Beat one egg until very light, add one teaspoonful of sugar, beat a few minutes longer, and stir into the corn-starch. Cook one minute, stirring well, add one fourth of a teaspoonful of lemon extract, remove from the fire.

Beat a few minutes with a wire spoon and pour into a mould.

When cold, turn out on a dish, place candied cherries, or any other candied fruit or rich preserves, around the edge, and serve with cream sweetened to taste and flavored with a teaspoonful of sherry or lemon extract.

Be exact in measuring the milk and corn-starch, as a little more or less will spoil the pudding.

Smooth off the corn-starch with a knife-blade, to be sure that the spoonfuls are level ones.

TEA.

Put into a dry, heated earthenware teapot two level teaspoonfuls of tea, and pour on one pint of freshly boiling water.

Cover and set on a hot part of the stove where it will not boil but simply keep hot for ten minutes; then strain into a heated china teapot for the table.

Throw away the tea-leaves; they have been exhausted of all that is fit for use.

V.

Soup.

Roast lamb. Grape jelly.
Escalloped potatoes.
White turnips with cream sauce.
Bread and butter.

Salad.
Chicory or lettuce.
Cheese sandwiches.

Orange tapioca pudding with whipped cream.

Tea or coffee. Dates and English walnuts.

SOUP.

Take one and a half cupfuls of clear soup-stock, heat, and add the yolk of a hot hard-boiled egg which has been mashed to a smooth paste with a level teaspoonful of flour and a heaping teaspoonful of butter.

Stir this well into the boiling stock, cook for a minute, add salt and pepper to taste, and serve.

The white of the egg may be sliced and added if desired.

If the soup is lumpy after the paste is added, strain before serving.

If more onion flavor is liked, grate in a few drops.

CLEAR SOUP-STOCK.

In the family where soup is considered a daily necessity, the housekeeper will find that a soup-stock kept in bulk, ready for use, will be not only of great convenience, but a saving of time and labor as well.

The following is a delicious white stock which will keep a week in cold weather.

Soak over night in two quarts of cold water, one cupful of split peas. Next morning add a quarter of a pound of delicately browned fried salt pork (do not use the grease), one pound of stewing veal from the neck, dredged lightly with flour, one chopped onion, one chopped carrot, several sprigs of parsley, a pinch of cayenne pepper, and one teaspoonful of sugar. Set on the back of the range to heat slowly, and cook for five or six hours, closely covered, very gently. Add salt to taste, the last half-hour.

When done, pour into a soup-strainer set over a deep dish, and let it drain.

Put that which remains in the sieve back into the pot, add a cup of hot water and boil ten or fifteen minutes, then drain again, throwing away that which remains in the strainer. There should be something over a quart of liquor.

When cold, carefully remove the clear layer of jelly on top and use it for clear soup.

The thick part remaining in the bottom of the dish may be converted into a tomato soup by adding the same quantity of tomatoes which have been cooked and strained.

This makes a fine thick soup for luncheon or for a dinner when cold sliced roasts are used.

The addition of a turkey or chicken carcass makes this stock still more delicious. Break the bones into small pieces, cover with cold water, and boil for several hours. Strain and add to the stock.

A fine large turkey carcass will yield a pint of jelly, and a chicken carcass half a cupful.

Hard-boiled eggs, tomatoes, rice, noodles, or milk and macaroni, may be added to the clear stock as desired, making agreeable changes from day to day.

ROAST LAMB.

Take a chop two inches thick from the prime part of a fine leg of lamb. Dust it with pepper, dredge with flour, and put it into a hot spider to brown on all sides over a hot fire ; or broil it over a clear fierce fire. This seals up the juices, preventing their escape while roasting.

The meat should cook only long enough to become brown.

Do not puncture with a fork, but use a broad knife for turning.

Time, from five to eight minutes.

Put a meat-rack or wire tea-stand into a dripping-pan or pie-pan, lay the meat on it, and roast in a moderate oven from thirty to fifty minutes. Take it out at the expiration of thirty minutes and cut a small deep gash in the centre; pry apart, and if not cooked to suit, return to the oven and bake longer.

The juice should be red, but the meat a brownish pink.

Dust with salt, and put it on a small warmed platter.

Mix a rounded tablespoonful of flour with two tablespoonfuls of cold water, and stir this into the gravy in the pan; add a half-cupful of boiling water, stir well, boil a few minutes, add salt to taste, and serve either in a gravy-boat or pour it over the meat on the platter.

Serve as soon as possible, garnished with parsley.

In carving, serve only the choice portions cut in wedges.

Reserve the poorer part and bones for a second meal, which is prepared in this way: Cut into dice, dredge with flour, cover with boiling water, and stew gently, closely covered, for an hour, or longer if necessary. Add any gravy which was left, salt to taste, take out the bones, add two tablespoonfuls of capers, and, after boiling up once, serve. If there was no gravy, make some by blending together one tablespoonful of butter and one teaspoonful of flour, and stir into the stew before adding the capers. Add also a little water if needed.

ESCALLOPED POTATOES.

Slice in thin slices two cupfuls of cold boiled or baked potatoes. Dust with flour, salt, and black pepper, put into an earthen baking-dish, distribute a dessert-spoonful of butter over the top in small pieces, and fill the dish with milk to just cover the top of the potatoes.

Bake in a moderate oven for half an hour. The top should be a delicate brown, and the potatoes a little creamy. If baked too long or too fast they will be hard and dry.

Serve in the dish in which they were baked.

TURNIPS WITH CREAM SAUCE.

Wash and peel two medium-sized white turnips. Slice in inch pieces and cook in boiling water just enough to cover, with half a teaspoonful of salt. When tender, drain and put them in a hot vegetable dish. Make a sauce of a dessert-spoonful of butter, one of flour, and a pinch of salt blended together.

Add half a cupful of hot milk, boil up, and pour over the turnips.

Sprinkle with pepper and send to the table.

SALAD OF CHICORY OR LETTUCE WITH FRENCH DRESSING.

Wash and pull apart a crisp head of chicory and serve with a dressing of three scant tablespoonfuls of vinegar (real cider vinegar), one saltspoonful of salt, a pinch of cayenne pepper, and six tablespoonfuls of olive-oil.

Pass, with this, small cheese sandwiches made in this way:

Grate three tablespoonfuls of cheese, add one teaspoonful of butter and a pinch of cayenne pepper; work into a paste with a knife-blade and spread on the end of a loaf of bread. Cut this off in a slice a quarter of an inch thick, remove the crust and double together, cutting the sandwiches about three inches square. Use old English cheese.

ORANGE TAPIOCA PUDDING WITH WHIPPED CREAM.

Put two heaping tablespoonfuls of flake tapioca in a cloth and pound it to the size of small peas. Rinse in cold water and soak over night in a cupful of cold water. Next morning add an eighth of a teaspoonful of salt, three tablespoonfuls of sugar, and two thirds of a cupful of orange juice.

Add more sugar if the oranges are very sour.

Cook until clear (about five minutes after the boiling begins), stirring constantly to prevent scorching.

Pour into a glass dish and, when cold, heap whipped cream on top.

Serve with sponge cake, lady-fingers, or delicate crackers.

The cream is prepared in this way:

Put into an ice-cold bowl four tablespoonfuls of ice-cold cream and whip with a wire spoon for about ten minutes, or until it is stiff, then add a few grains of salt, one heaping tablespoonful of confectioner's sugar, and either a pinch of grated orange rind or a quarter of a teaspoonful of vanilla extract.

To get the juice from oranges, cut crosswise and take out with a spoon the pulp in each section, rejecting seeds and all tough portions.

The cream sold from the dairies where a "separator" is used is easily whipped.

It is often called "new process cream" and does not need to be drained after being beaten stiff. If the cream will not whip readily it may be used plain with a little sugar and gelatine in this way:

SUBSTITUTE FOR WHIPPED CREAM.

Put one even teaspoonful of gelatine in three teaspoonfuls of cold water, soak ten minutes, then melt in a warm place until it is liquid.

Whip for five or six minutes with a wire spoon in a warm room, when the gelatine will become stiff froth.

Add five tablespoonfuls of rich cream, very cold, one tablespoonful confectioner's sugar, a few grains of salt, and flavoring to suit.

Pour immediately over the pudding, which must be quite cold.

VI.

Potato purée.
Fried ham. Cream gravy.
Fried hominy.
Stewed corn or parsnip patties.
Tomatoes stewed in butter.
Escalloped oysters.
Cold slaw. Crackers. Cheese.
Lemon meringue pie.
Tea or coffee.

Alternative : Mutton pot-roast. Cherry pudding.

PURÉE OF POTATOES.

To a heaping cupful of mashed potatoes add a tablespoonful of butter rubbed with a teaspoonful of flour. Stir into this a pint of boiling milk (carefully, to prevent lumping), add a teaspoonful of onion juice, half a teaspoonful of salt, boil up, and strain.

Serve with minced parsley and squares of bread toasted brown in the oven.

FRIED HAM.

One slice of ham three quarters of an inch thick.

Cut off the rind, put ham into a smoking-hot spider, and fry each side one minute. Remove to a cooler part of the range and fry each side ten minutes; sprinkle with a teaspoonful of granulated sugar after turning the last time.

Put the meat on a platter, pour into the spider two thirds of a cup of milk, stir the sediment, boil once, and pour over the ham.

If ham is suspected of being too salt, soak a few hours in the milk which should afterwards be used for the gravy.

FRIED HOMINY.

Slice cold boiled hominy, dredge with flour, and fry brown in a little hot salt-pork drippings.

Serve buttered and peppered.

STEWED CORN.

Grate a heaping cupful of green uncooked corn, add one fourth of a cupful of rich milk, a dust of flour, pepper and salt to taste, and a teaspoonful of butter. Boil up once and take from the fire. If cooked corn is used, do not boil it, but add to the milk, etc., which must be boiling, stir, and serve as soon as it is hot.

Canned corn may be used in the same way.

PARSNIP PATTIES.

Wash and boil till very tender in salted boiling water, one large parsnip. Scrape off the skin and mash to a pulp while hot; there should be a cupful.

Add one heaping teaspoonful of butter, one of flour, and half an even teaspoonful of salt. Stir well, and add the yolk of an egg, and mould into four little flat cakes.

If the mixture sticks, dip the hands into cold water, shake off the drops, and proceed.

Dip the cakes into powdered cracker crumbs, and when cold fry a delicate brown in hot butter.

It will take a teaspoonful of butter for each side. Do not cook longer than actually necessary to brown and heat through, or the egg will harden and the cakes lose their creaminess.

TOMATOES STEWED IN BUTTER.

Put a lump of butter the size of a large nutmeg into a saucepan, dredge with half a teaspoonful of flour, and on this, carefully, so as not to displace the butter, pour two thirds of a cup of canned tomatoes or a full cup of sliced fresh tomatoes.

Sprinkle with salt and pepper and a teaspoonful of flour, cover, and cook gently twenty-five minutes.

Do not stir while cooking, and use an earthenware dish that may be sent to the table.

Butter, flour, and tomatoes should all remain in separate masses, blending only at the point of contact.

ESCALLOPED OYSTERS.

One solid pint of oysters.

On the bottom of an earthen- or agate-ware baking-dish put a layer of whole sea-foam or milk crackers, liberally spread with sweet butter.

Cover with a layer of oysters, then one of buttered whole crackers, and another layer of oysters.

Pour in a half-pint of milk, sweet and rich; poor milk is apt to curdle.

Add to any liquor that remains, enough rolled cracker to make a paste with a tablespoonful of melted butter, and spread over the top of the oysters.

If not enough liquor remains, use milk instead. Bake in a hot oven long enough for the milk to reach the boiling point; twenty minutes will probably suffice.

The top should be brown. Serve in the baking-dish.

COLD SLAW.

Shave the crisp inner leaves of cabbage as

thinly as possible, cover with ice-water, and set in a cold place until wanted.

Drain, and serve with any preferred dressing.

LEMON MERINGUE PIE.

Line a pie-pan of medium size with pie-crust and bake; then fill with the following mixture:

Beat the yolks of two large fresh eggs with four tablespoonfuls of sugar, a pinch of salt, the juice of a whole lemon, and the grated rind of half.

Mix one even teaspoonful of corn-starch with a tablespoonful of melted butter and stir it into one cupful of boiling milk; cook and stir for a minute, and when cold pour slowly over the egg mixture.

Stir all together and bake in the baked crust about fifteen minutes. Take from the oven and spread over the whites of the eggs which have been frothed and beaten with four tablespoonfuls of sugar and a tiny pinch of salt, return to the oven, and brown a few minutes, being careful not to burn.

Serve cold.

MUTTON OVEN POT-ROAST.

Two slices, each one inch thick, from the middle part of the leg, either raw or cold roast.

Trim off the outer edge of fat, put one slice on a meat-rack in an earthen baking-dish, dust with flour and pepper, and dot with butter. Lay the second slice on this and treat in the same way. Pour over half a cup of boiling water, cover closely, and bake in a slow oven two hours. Sprinkle with salt, and send to the table in the baking-dish, after removing the rack. Mint or wine sauce.

CHERRY PUDDING (STEAMED).

Stone a pound of cherries, put them in a deep quart bowl, and scatter two tablespoonfuls of sugar and two of water over them.

Make a crust of one cupful of flour, sifted with one teaspoonful of baking-powder and half a teaspoonful of salt, and chop with half a cupful of kidney suet.

Mix with a scant half-cupful of ice-water, pat into shape, and lay on top of the cherries.

Steam in a steamer one hour, and serve on a deep platter with rich sauce.

The whipped-egg sauce may be used.

VII.

Consommé.
Roast chicken, stuffed.
Fried rice.
Escalloped tomatoes.
Parsnips browned in butter.
Radishes or celery.
Currant or grape jelly.
Lettuce or celery with French dressing,
or
Oyster salad. Cheese. Crackers.
Strawberry shortcake.
Tea or coffee.
Nuts. Bonbons.

CONSOMMÉ.

This is a clear soup and the basis of nearly all soups.

By adding different vegetables and flavorings one has the tomato, julienne, rice, macaroni, etc.

Consommé is only another term for stock or bouillon : it is made of meat, water, and vegetables, sometimes spices, and strained through a strainer set over a napkin wrung out of hot water.

Take two pounds of soup-beef and a bone, extra.

Soak for two hours in two quarts of cold water to draw out the juices. Add a sliced carrot, an onion, a few celery stalks, and boil slowly until the meat is in shreds. There should be one quart of liquor after straining. Season and set away to get cold, when skim off any fat there may be on top.

Heat one cupful of this for two portions, and serve with small crackers.

A few sprigs of parsley or a slice of lemon or a poached egg in each portion makes a change.

The meat is now useless; if soup-meat is wanted for food it is better to buy what is called a "fresh plate piece," two pounds of which will make a quart of soup. Wipe off the meat with a cloth, pour on a quart of boiling water, bring to a quick boil for a few minutes, then merely simmer on a cool part of the stove, covered, for four hours, or until the bones drop out. Put the meat on a platter, make a gravy of one cupful of the liquor mixed with a teaspoonful of flour, with pepper and salt, and pour over.

Add vegetables and a cupful of water to the liquor, cook and strain, and set away for next day's soup.

The vegetables may be served with the meat.

ROAST CHICKEN.

Select a fine fat yellow fowl weighing four or five pounds (a thin white-skinned chicken is apt to be tasteless and tough), and ask the butcher to draw it. Cut off the legs, wings, and neck, and put away for a fricassee.

Rinse the body of the chicken quickly in cold water inside and out, wipe dry, and fill with the following stuffing:

Put a quart of stale bread-crumbs into a vessel with a cover, pour in a cup of cold water, drain, and steam, covered, in a hot oven for half an hour.

Then add a quarter of a teaspoonful of black pepper, half a teaspoonful of salt, two heaping teaspoonfuls of thyme, and one of chopped onion. Work this into a paste with a tablespoonful of butter. Add a few spoonfuls more of water if needed.

Fill the chicken and sew up with coarse darning-cotton. Dredge with flour and black pepper, place upon a meat-rack in a deep saucepan or pot with a close-fitting cover, add half a cup of boiling water, and bake from two to four hours in a moderate oven.

The time will depend on the toughness of the fowl. Leave off the cover the last half-hour, and at this time sprinkle with salt. Meanwhile cook the heart, liver, and gizzard half an hour in a cupful of boiling water.

Take out the gizzard and put it with the parts reserved for the fricassee.

Chop heart and liver, mix with them a tablespoonful of flour and half a teaspoonful of salt, stir into the water they boiled in, cook a few minutes, and add any gravy there may be in the roasting-pot.

For the fricassee wipe the pieces (legs, wings, etc.) with a damp cloth, dredge with flour and black pepper, place in a stew-pan, pour on one and a half cups of boiling water, cover closely, and cook very gently from one to four hours, or until tender.

When done, blend a tablespoonful of flour with a lump of butter the size of an egg, add half a cupful of boiling water, the gizzard chopped very fine, salt to taste, cook with the chicken, and serve on a deep platter.

If the chicken is very fat, the butter will not be needed.

FRIED RICE.

Pack into a square pan two cupfuls of well-boiled rice. When cold, cut into inch-thick slices, dredge with flour, and fry brown in a spoonful of hot butter or salt-pork drippings.

Serve with a lump of butter on each piece, and dust with black pepper.

ESCALLOPED TOMATOES.

Use either a small baking-dish or individual moulds (cups will do). Skin and slice two fine ripe tomatoes, and lay them in a dish with alternate layers of fine cracker-crumbs, pepper, salt, and bits of butter. A teaspoonful of butter for each tomato is about right.

Sprinkle with cracker-crumbs and bake half an hour in a hot oven. Serve in the baking-dish. Canned tomatoes may be used, but are not so good as fresh ones.

BUTTERED PARSNIPS.

Boil in salted water until tender one fine large parsnip.

Scrape and cut in halves lengthwise.

Dredge with a little salt, flour, and pepper, and fry brown in a spoonful of butter.

OYSTER SALAD.

Dip six freshly opened medium-sized oysters in cracker-crumbs, and fry a delicate brown in a spoonful of hot sweet butter.

Lay on a plate to get cold, then cut them into half-inch pieces and mix with six tablespoonfuls of finely chopped crisp white celery. Put this in the salad bowl, first rubbing the inside of the bowl with a slice of raw onion, and set where it will get very cold.

Just before serving make the dressing.

Whip to a stiff froth a fourth of a cupful of sour cream. Beat the yolk of one egg with a pinch each of salt, mustard, cayenne, and sugar; add one spoonful of olive-oil and then the whipped cream. Add more salt if necessary, and a spoonful of either lemon juice or cider vinegar; the size of the spoonfuls should be governed by the acidity of the cream.

Pour over the salad and serve.

STRAWBERRY SHORTCAKE.

Sift together half a cupful of flour, half a rounded teaspoonful of baking-powder, and a large pinch of salt. Cut into this a lump of table butter the size of half an egg, and add one fourth of a cup of milk. Spread this paste on a jelly-cake pan and bake fifteen or twenty minutes in a hot oven, or bake in muffin rings. Spread, when done, liberally with butter, add the fruit, and serve either hot or cold.

Prepare the berries in the following way:

An hour before dinner pick over and rinse quickly two cupfuls of fine juicy strawberries, and cover with a cupful of sugar; set in a cool place until wanted. Just before the shortcake goes to the table, spread over it one cupful of mashed berries, and put on top the berries which have been standing in sugar.

Serve with cream, or make a sauce as follows:

Boil a cupful of milk, pour it upon the yolk of an egg beaten with one teaspoonful of sugar, add a few grains of salt, and set over a boiling tea-kettle about two minutes, stirring constantly.

The white of the egg may be frothed and added if liked. Serve hot or cold.

Canned cherries or peaches may take the place of the strawberries.

VIII.

Broth with lemon.
Stuffed leg of lamb.
Potatoes with cream sauce.
Green peas. Cape May omelette.
Bread and butter. Grape jelly.
Olives.
Salad of lettuce or cabbage with a boiled dressing.
Saltine crackers. Cheese.
Loaf cake with cut fruit.
Berries or canned fruit.
Tea or coffee. Nuts and cream candy.

BROTH.

Dredge with flour and cover with cold water the bone taken from a leg of lamb. Add one clove, an inch piece of stick cinnamon, a few inches of carrot, parsnip, and one onion.

Heat slowly and boil gently until the bones drop apart, which will be at the end of several hours; there should be a generous pint of broth after straining and skimming off the fat.

Add a few sprigs of parsley, salt and pepper, return to the pot, boil up, and serve with a thin slice of lemon in each portion.

If a larger amount of broth is wanted, add a part of the extreme lower end of the leg to the bone when putting on to cook; this also should be dredged with flour. One pound of meat will yield a pint of rich broth.

ROAST LAMB.

Order a small leg of lamb, weighing about five pounds, boned and trimmed. From the large end have two slices cut for broiling, and put on ice for next day's breakfast. Have two thirds of the small end cut off also, and reserved for a stew; the bone is for soup.

The portion left is the prime part to be used for the roast. Pour a cupful of boiling water over a pint of stale bread-crumbs, and pour off immediately; cover the bread closely, and set in a warm place to steam for about twenty-five minutes.

Add a piece of butter the size of half an egg, a salt-spoon of salt, the same of pepper, and mix; a little more water may be needed to make the stuffing pliable.

Broil the meat on every side over a fierce fire, or fry in a smoking-hot frying-pan just long enough to seal up the juices; place it on a small rack in a dripping-pan, and press the stuffing into the cavity made by the removal of the bone. Cover with a piece of the sheet of fat accompanying the lamb, dredge with flour, pour into the pan a cup of boiling water, and roast in a hot oven for half an hour.

If the rack is not high enough to admit of a cup of water, put in less, as the water must not touch the meat.

When done, dredge liberally with salt and pepper, and serve on a heated platter.

Pour off the grease from the gravy in the pan, add a pinch of salt, and a teaspoonful of flour blended with a little cold water, boil up, and serve in a gravy-boat.

If preferred, a mint sauce may take the place of the gravy, or, if mint is not at hand, a wine sauce.

When either of these sweet sauces are used, omit the grape jelly.

Next day the remains of the lamb may be sliced and made into cutlets. Dip them first into beaten egg, and then in bread-crumbs or cracker dust, and fry quickly in hot butter.

Fry just long enough to heat thoroughly, or the meat will be tough and fit only for the stew-pot.

For another meal, cut that which remains into dice, cover with boiling water, and stew one hour; season with salt, and add flour and capers, or serve with dumplings.

Lamb's kidneys may be added, also a tablespoonful of fried salt pork, or, in time of green peas, a cupful added to the gravy is a great improvement.

For mint sauce, pour half a cupful of boiling water on a tablespoonful of green mint (chopped). Add two tablespoonfuls of sugar, boil up, and serve with or without a spoonful of vinegar. For wine sauce, melt one teaspoonful of grape jelly over a teakettle, add one tablespoonful of sherry, and serve hot.

BOILED POTATOES.

Wash, peel, and cut in half-inch slices, two medium-sized potatoes, and rinse in cold water. Cover with boiling water, and cook gently, so as not to break, until a fork will pierce them easily. Then pour off the water, uncover for an instant, replace the lid, and holding it securely shake the pot violently up and down once. Now partly remove the cover, and set the pot on the stove for a few minutes to allow the potatoes to dry and become flaky. Then put them in a hot vegetable dish, sprinkle with salt, and pour over a sauce made as follows: Stir a heaping tablespoonful of butter to a cream, add a rounded dessert-spoonful of flour, a fourth of a teaspoonful of salt, beat well, and add a cupful of boiling milk. Boil gently, about ten minutes, adding a tablespoonful of finely minced parsley, and a dust of pepper. Serve at once.

GREEN PEAS.

Peas will take from twenty to forty minutes to cook, according to size and age.

Boil in two cups of boiling water, with an even teaspoonful of salt, three cups of peas, which are fresh and crisp.

Do not wash them at all, and see that they are not shelled long before using.

If the water cooks away, add more from the boiling teakettle, just enough to keep them covered.

When done, add pepper, dredge in a little flour, and stir in a tablespoonful of butter. Serve in sauce-plates.

If preferred, they may be boiled down very dry, and poured around the lamb; in which case a portion should be served with each plate.

CAPE MAY OMELETTE.

Pour one third of a cup of cold milk on half a cup of stale bread-crumbs; if the crumbs are very dry, a little more milk may be required.

Beat well one egg with half an even teaspoonful of salt, a dust of pepper, and a tablespoonful of butter, melted. Add half a cup of green corn, grated, or the same amount of canned corn, and mix with the crumbs and milk.

Bake in a buttered earthen dish in a hot oven,

just long enough to set the egg and brown the top, from ten to fifteen minutes.

Be careful about the quantity of milk, as too much will make the omelette thin, while it will be stiff if too little is used.

To be right, it should be about as stiff as light mashed potatoes.

CABBAGE SALAD.

Shave very fine half a pint of cabbage; only the tender inner parts should be used.

Make a dressing of the yolk of one egg beaten with one third of a teaspoonful of flour, the same of salt, and a pinch of sugar, and a dust of cayenne pepper.

Add two tablespoonfuls of boiling water and cook and stir over a boiling teakettle until thick; then add a tablespoonful of cider vinegar, a tablespoonful of cream or milk, and a teaspoonful of butter.

Beat until cold and mix with the cabbage, or pour over lettuce leaves and serve in a salad bowl. Oil may be used instead of butter, if preferred.

LOAF CAKE.

Half a cupful of butter, one cupful granulated sugar, three eggs, half a cupful of lukewarm water, one and a half cupfuls flour, one and a half teaspoonfuls baking-powder, one teaspoonful flavoring, half a scant teaspoonful salt.

Beat the butter to a cream with the hand, add the sugar, and mix until it is a creamy mass.

Add the yolks of the eggs, beating (still with the hand) for fully five minutes, then add by degrees the water. Beat from five to ten minutes and put in the flavoring. Measure the flour carefully, *lifting* it lightly in the cup, add the baking-powder and salt, and sift four times.

Beat the flour into the egg mixture with a spoon, putting it in by degrees, about a third at a time.

Beat thoroughly for five minutes, then grease the baking-pan; then beat the cake again for a few minutes; this alternate beating and resting improves it very much.

Whisk the whites of the eggs, which have been standing in a cool place, and, as soon as they are stiff, beat up the cake batter once more and fold or cut them in lightly. The cake should only be beaten enough at this stage to mix in the whites of the eggs, as long beating after they are in always tends to make cake tough.

Pour into a paper-lined tin (fill a little over half full), smooth the top evenly, and bake in a moderate oven from fifty to sixty minutes. In baking see that the fire is right before adding flour to the cake, and after it goes into the oven do not slam doors nor open windows to make a draught across the stove. A jar or draught will often cause cakes to fall.

When looking into the oven, open the door only part way (to prevent the escape of hot air), and always open and close it gently.

When the cake is done it will be a beautiful golden brown, slightly raised in the centre, with the edges fallen away from the sides of the pan.

This cake will keep for a week in a closely covered stone jar and is almost equal to pound cake in closeness and richness.

Do not use milk instead of water, and be exact in measuring everything. The butter should be pressed closely into the cup in order to get the full quantity.

This same batter may be used for layer cake. Do not fill the pans quite full; and smooth the top of each with a knife-blade, or the cakes will not be even when baked.

Have a quick oven and turn the cakes, when done, upon a clean cloth, with the inverted pans over them so they will keep moist until ready for the filling, which may be either chocolate, jelly, or custard.

Layer-cake batter needs but little beating after the flour is added.

IX.

Macaroni soup.

Chicken browned in butter;
Giblet gravy.   Currant jelly.

Hashed potatoes with parsley.
Lima beans.
Bread and butter. Olives.

Lettuce; French dressing.
Philadelphia cream cheese.
Educator crackers.

Jelly with preserved pineapple and whipped cream.

Lady-fingers or sponge cake.

Tea or coffee.   Nut cream candy.

MACARONI SOUP.

Use stock, but if none is at hand, then, several hours before dinner, put into an earthen pot half a pound of raw chopped soup beef, a small bone, and a generous half-pint of cold water. Set on a cool part of the range for three hours where it will heat gradually; then bring to a boil and cook gently for half an hour with one chopped onion, two inches of carrot, and a sprig of parsley.

Strain through a soup-strainer, and again through a piece of old table-linen wet in cold water, if a clear soup is desired. If the soup has boiled away, add enough boiling water to make a generous half-pint and set away in a cold place.

Half an hour before it is wanted, break into a cup of boiling water a heaping tablespoonful of macaroni and cook until tender. Remove the cake of fat from the soup, add one third of a teaspoonful of salt, a dust of pepper, a pinch of sugar, and one clove, heat, and pour over the macaroni just before serving. There should be a cupful and a half of soup.

The coarse end of porter-house steak and its bone can be used for this soup, and also the ends from lamb chops.

CHICKEN BROWNED IN BUTTER; GIBLET GRAVY.

Cut wings and legs from a fine fat chicken weighing four or five pounds.

Singe over a flame to burn off hairs and the little feathers which cannot be plucked out.

Rinse quickly in cold water, wipe dry, and put into a saucepan or frying-pan in which a lump of butter the size of an egg is heating.

The bottom of the pan should be broad enough to admit of all the pieces of chicken being spread upon it at one time.

Dust each piece with a little flour and pepper and fry delicately upon both sides for a few minutes: then cover the saucepan closely, set on a cool part of the stove where it will only simmer very gently, and cook from half an hour to two hours, according to the age of the fowl.

Turn each piece occasionally and keep constant watch to see that the heat is not too great, as burning would impart bitterness to the gravy.

The chicken when done should be a rich golden brown and so tender that the meat can easily be twisted apart with a fork.

Place on a hot platter and garnish either with parsley or watercress.

Do not season with salt until ready to go to the table.

Stir into the saucepan one teaspoonful of flour, one fourth of a teaspoonful of salt, and half a cup of boiling water.

Chop the heart and half of the liver, and add this with a little pepper. Cook gently for fifteen minutes and serve in a small gravy-boat.

If the butter in the pan should have become scorched, do not use it for the gravy, but take a fresh supply.

The body of the chicken can be roasted

another day, using the gizzard and the other half of the liver for gravy.

The grease from salt pork may be used instead of butter, and if the chicken is known to be old it may be steamed for an hour, to make it tender, before frying.

HASHED POTATOES WITH MINCED PARSLEY.

Stir together in a small frying-pan one even dessert-spoonful of flour, one teaspoonful of butter, one fourth of a teaspoonful of salt, and, when hot, add a third of a cup of rich milk; stir constantly and cook for a minute, then add two even cupfuls of thinly sliced, cold, baked or boiled potatoes. Stir lightly so that every piece may be coated with the sauce, add a tablespoonful of minced parsley, and do not stir again. Cover and cook gently a few minutes, then dust with pepper and serve.

LIMA BEANS (DRIED.)

Soak half a cupful of dried lima beans for twenty-four hours in one pint of cold water. Rinse thoroughly, and cook gently for two hours in a cup of cold water: if cooked fast they will break and become mushy.

When tender, add a lump of butter the size of an English walnut, a quarter of a teaspoonful of salt, and a sprinkle of pepper. If too dry, add one or two spoonfuls of milk just before serving.

LETTUCE; FRENCH DRESSING.

Wash with care, in cold water, the tender inner leaves of a crisp head of lettuce.

Shake out the water, put in a salad bowl, and serve with the following dressing: Mix one tablespoonful of real cider vinegar with three tablespoonfuls of olive-oil, a generous pinch of salt, a tiny one of red pepper, and a dust of black pepper. Toss the leaves about in this, being careful that each is well coated.

Pass crackers and cheese with this course.

JELLY WITH PRESERVED PINEAPPLE AND WHIPPED CREAM.

Soak four even teaspoonfuls of gelatine in two tablespoonfuls of cold water for ten minutes. Add the juice of half a lemon, granulated sugar to taste, one cup of boiling water, and four tablespoonfuls of juice from some canned pineapples.

Cut into dice two slices of the pineapple and cook gently for fifteen minutes with two tablespoonfuls of sugar, being careful not to let it burn.

Spread this on the bottom of a glass dish, and pour the gelatine mixture over it.

When ice-cold and hard, heap on top four

tablespoonfuls of cream, which have been whipped with one teaspoonful of confectioner's sugar.

In warm weather use three tablespoonfuls less water in the jelly.

X.

Purée of green peas.

Veal pot-pie (raised crust).
Cauliflower fritters.
Baked tomatoes.
Bread and butter.   Olives.

Green corn on the cob.

Lemon pudding.

Tea or coffee.   Chocolate creams.

PURÉE OF GREEN PEAS.

Barely cover with boiling water one cupful of fresh green peas, adding more from the boiling teakettle as the peas become dry.

When tender, press through a coarse sieve or mash very fine, add two scant cupfuls of boiling milk, and to this a teaspoonful of butter blended with one of flour. Boil a few minutes, add salt to taste, a dust of pepper, strain if lumpy, and serve with small squares of bread browned in the oven.

VEAL POT-PIE. (YEAST CRUST.)

Put one pound of stewing veal lightly dredged with flour into one pint of boiling water. Add two tablespoonfuls of chopped salt pork fried a rich brown (not the grease) and a piece of red pepper pod the size of a thumb-nail or a pinch of cayenne. Cover the pot and stew gently for three hours, then add a dessert-spoonful of flour and an even teaspoonful of salt to half a cupful of melted butter, stir well, and mix with the veal.

Boil a few minutes, add a half-cup of boiling water, stir and boil up, then set away until next day in a very cold place.

Veal is always improved by standing a day in its juices, being sweeter and firmer.

Six hours before dinner mix the sponge for the crust.

Take a half-teaspoonful of salt, the same of sugar, a half-cup of warm water, a half-teaspoonful of butter, and one fourth of a yeast-cake. Melt and mix all together and stir in one cupful of flour sifted after measuring.

Let it rise to double its bulk in a temperature of about ninety degrees: this will take about three hours. Make into biscuits by rolling small pieces between the floured palms, and set to rise again in the same temperature, always keeping the vessel closely covered.

At the end of this time the rolls should have become three times the original size and are now ready for the steamer: steam one hour: break apart, place on a deep platter, and pour the stew (which has been getting hot but not cooking for the past half-hour) over them.

If more gravy is needed, melt and brown slightly one tablespoonful of butter, add a teaspoonful of flour, a little salt and pepper, and half a cup of boiling water. Lamb may be used instead of veal, and should be cooked in the same way.

Get stewing lamb, and remove the fat, if there is any, before cooking.

Buy large, old veal.

CAULIFLOWER FRITTERS.

Boil for twenty minutes in boiling salted water three cupfuls of cauliflower.

Take from the fire, mash fine with a fork, add a tablespoonful of butter, and form into little flat cakes. When cold, dip them in a batter made of beaten egg, a pinch of salt, a tablespoonful of milk, and a teaspoonful of flour.

Fry to a light brown in a spoonful of hot butter, or, if preferred, in salt-pork drippings. Cook the fritters the last thing, as they should be served at once.

BAKED TOMATOES.

Skin ripe tomatoes by pouring boiling water over them to cover.

Place them in an earthenware dish, put on each tomato a walnut of butter, a large pinch of salt, and a dust of pepper, and dredge with flour. Cover the dish closely and bake in a moderately hot oven from one and a half to two hours or longer, according to the size and ripeness of the tomatoes.

Remove the cover and bake fifteen minutes to half an hour longer. If there is any juice at this time, dip it out of the dish, and add to it butter, flour, and salt enough to make a rich sauce; pour this over the tomatoes and serve hot in the baking-dish.

If there is no juice (which will be the case if the tomatoes are not particularly fine and ripe, or if they have cooked in an oven that is too hot or too cool), make a sauce of butter and flour stirred smooth with a little boiling water added.

Each tomato of medium size will require half a teaspoonful of butter, the same of flour, and two dessert-spoonfuls of boiling water, with a pinch each of salt and pepper.

The tomatoes when done should be soft and juicy but not broken. They may be browned by sprinkling with bread crumbs and holding over them a hot stove-lid.

GREEN CORN ON THE COB.

Strip the husks and silk from two ears of freshly pulled corn.

The sooner corn is eaten after being gathered, the sweeter it is.

Steam in a steamer for twenty minutes, or boil ten minutes.

In either case serve soon, each ear wrapped in a small napkin.

To roast, lay on a gridiron over a clear but not fierce fire, turning over a little at a time as the surface becomes browned: time about twenty-five minutes. Wrap in a napkin and eat with butter, salt, and pepper the same as boiled corn. The napkin is used to protect the fingers from the heat. Serve as a separate course.

LEMON PUDDING (MERINGUE).

Heat two thirds of a cup of rich milk, add an even tablespoonful of sugar, and the same of melted butter. Pour this over a cupful of bread crumbs, two days old, freed from crust, and, without stirring, set it on the stove to keep hot, but not to cook, while the yolk of an egg is being beaten with an even tablespoonful of sugar, the grated rind of a quarter of a lemon, and the juice of a fourth of it.

Add a pinch of salt, stir, and then pour in one third of a cupful of cold milk.

Pour this over the bread, and bake in a hot oven a few minutes.

Whip the white of the egg to a stiff froth, add the juice from one fourth of the lemon with one third of a cupful of sugar, spread over the hot pudding, and brown in the oven from eight to ten minutes.

Serve cold the day it is made.

The dish must be a third larger than the pudding to prevent the meringue from overflowing.

BAKED MEAT PIE.

The preceding dinner may be varied by serving a meat pie instead of the veal pot-pie, in which case a strawberry jelly may take the place of the lemon meringue.

For the meat pie, use any meat from roast or poultry, and if it is not perfectly tender dredge it (one cupful) with flour, barely cover with boiling water, and simmer from one to three hours, or fry it in a closely covered saucepan, just allowing it to simmer (using a thin slice of fat salt pork in the bottom of the pan to furnish fat) for the same length of time.

Put the meat, cut into dice, in a deep baking-dish, fill up with gravy, cover with the following crust, and bake half an hour in a hot oven.

Take half a cupful of flour, sift it with half a

teaspoonful of baking-powder, a salt-spoonful of salt, and chop with it a lump of suet the size of a hen's egg.

Mix in four tablespoonfuls of ice-cold water, roll out very lightly, place lightly on top of the meat, and get it into the oven as quickly as possible.

If no gravy remained from the roast, make some after directions previously given.

STRAWBERRY JELLY.

Soak for half an hour three tablespoonfuls of gelatine in one cup of cold water, with the juice of a quarter of a lemon. Stem and mash a quart box of juicy strawberries and strain through a coarse cloth wrung out of cold water : squeeze out all the juice possible. Add five tablespoonfuls of confectioner's sugar, a few grains of salt, and set the gelatine on the stove, stirring until it is all melted.

Then add the strawberry juice and taste to see if more sugar or lemon is needed.

When cold, but before it stiffens, whip with an egg-beater until nothing is visible but a froth : this will take from ten minutes to half an hour. Now add the frothed white of an egg, whip a few minutes longer, and set on ice for several hours in the dish in which it is to be served.

Whipped cream is an addition to this jelly but it is very nice without.

To be right, one third should be a rose colored foam, resting upon a clear rose jelly.

Currant juice may be used instead of lemon.

XI.

Split-pea soup.
Pot roast, top sirloin.
Mashed potatoes.
Tomatoes on toast.
Watercress.   Bread and butter.
Tapioca pudding.
Hard sauce.
Tea or coffee.
Dates.   English walnuts.

Serve cresses with the meat, or, if preferred, in a separate course with crackers and cheese.

SPLIT-PEA SOUP.

Wash half a cupful of split peas and soak them over night in a quart of cold water.

About noon put them, with the water they have soaked in, on a cool part of the stove, add two tablespoonfuls of chopped salt pork, fried brown (do not use the grease), a half-cupful of tomatoes, a few sprigs of parsely and celery stalks, and one onion, one small turnip, and a medium-sized carrot chopped fine.

Heat gradually and cook slowly until the peas are a mush, which will take several hours. Then add one half of the gravy from the pot roast, boil a few minutes, and strain through a soup-strainer. There should be a quart of soup. If the liquor has boiled away, add boiling water to the pot, cook a little longer, and strain. Salt and pepper to taste and serve with small oyster-crackers.

This quantity is enough for two meals. That which is left can be warmed up with a few spoonfuls of milk to thin it. Heat milk and soup in separate vessels and put together after taking from the fire. Add a little salt and some minced parsley.

POT-ROAST.
Top Sirloin (Two Pounds).

Trim off all the dried outer edges and brown on all sides in a hot spider over a hot fire to seal up the juices.

Dredge plentifully with flour and place the meat on a layer of thin slices of salt pork, or suet if preferred. Use an agate-ware pot and keep the meat closely covered so that the steam will not escape.

Set on a hot part of the stove until the fat

begins to fry vigorously, then place where it will only simmer.

Cook for two hours and a half, being careful that it does not burn. Suet especially is most disagreeable when burned, making the gravy quite unfit for use.

Be sure that the salt pork is fresh and sweet, as otherwise the dish will be ruined.

When done, take out the meat, dust it liberally with salt and a little pepper, and put it on a dish which can be covered, so that it will keep moist until ready to serve.

After taking out the pork, skim the fat from the gravy and put half of it in the soup as directed. Add to the remaining half a teaspoonful of flour mixed with a spoonful of cold water and a half-cupful of boiling water, salt to taste, and boil five minutes. If lumpy, strain through a wire strainer.

In serving the roast be sure to cut across the grain, and always observe the same rule when cutting meat for stews or pies, or to serve cold, sliced.

A delicious pie may be made from the remains of this roast for the following day. Cut up a heaping cupful of the meat into dice and put it into a small, deep pie-dish. Make a gravy of one heaping tablespoonful of butter, a tablespoonful of flour, half a teaspoonful of salt, pepper, and a cupful of boiling water. (Brown the butter before adding the other ingredients.) Pour this gravy over the meat, place on top a crust which has been previously baked, and set in the oven for fifteen or twenty minutes. Make the crust of one half cup of flour sifted with one fourth of a teaspoonful of salt, one fourth of a cup of lard (solid and cold), and two tablespoonfuls of ice-water. Roll out an eighth of an inch thick, spread on half a teaspoonful of butter, dust with flour, fold up into a ball and roll out again to the size and shape of the baking-dish, slash it once or twice, and bake in a hot oven. Handle the dough as little and as lightly as possible; have the hands cool and work quickly. The crust may be baked at any time so as to be in readiness when wanted.

MASHED POTATOES.

Wash, peel, and cook in enough boiling water to cover, three medium-sized potatoes.

When done a fork will pierce to the heart without resistance. Potatoes boil more quickly if cut in halves, but if small they do not need to be cut; try to have them of uniform size.

Drain off the water, take the lid off for a moment, slip it back, and, holding the pot and lid firmly together, shake up and down twice violently. This forces the steam to escape and makes the potatoes mealy, if it is possible for them to be so. Now pass through the potato press or mash thoroughly, until every lump disappears.

Add one third of a teaspoonful of salt, one teaspoonful of butter, and three tablespoonfuls of boiling milk.

Whip with a fork for two minutes and if not creamy enough add another spoonful of hot milk.

If too much milk is used the potatoes will be thin, if too little, they will not be creamy.

If possible use cream instead of milk.

Heap in a vegetable dish, put on top a lump of butter the size of a walnut, dust with pepper, and set in the oven until wanted for the table.

TOMATOES ON TOAST.

Skin two solid, ripe tomatoes, slice, dredge with flour, salt and pepper, and fry slowly in a teaspoonful of hot butter; they should be done in about ten minutes. Lift out carefully with a cake-turner and lay upon a thin slice of delicately toasted bread which has been freed from crust.

Add to the gravy in the pan an even tablespoonful of butter, one teaspoonful of flour, and two spoonfuls of milk or cream; cook a few minutes, salt and pepper lightly, pour over the tomatoes and toast, and serve.

If canned tomatoes are used, put a tablespoonful of butter in small lumps in the bottom of a saucepan, dredge lightly with flour, and pour over a scant cupful of canned tomatoes.

Add one fourth of a teaspoonful of salt, a dust of pepper and another sprinkling of flour, cover, and stew gently half an hour or longer without stirring. Pour over toast, and serve.

TAPIOCA PUDDING (BAKED).

Soak over night one even gill of flake tapioca in one cupful of cold water. An hour before dinner add half a cupful of cold milk, and heat gradually.

Beat up one egg with one tablespoonful of sugar, half a teaspoonful of salt, the grated rind of one third of a lemon, and pour upon this a half-cupful of boiling milk, stir well, and add to the tapioca.

Bake in a moderate oven about fifteen minutes; long cooking makes tapioca tough.

Serve hot with a sauce made of one scant cupful of confectioner's sugar, stirred with a lump of butter the size of a small egg and one teaspoonful of lemon juice.

The longer and harder this sauce is beaten the creamier it will be.

A gill measures one half of a cup. Be careful to have the measure exact, as too much tapioca will make the pudding stiff, and too much milk and water will make it insipid.

XII.

Celery soup.

Loin of lamb chops (broiled).
Baked potatoes.
Lemon marmalade.

Salted almonds.
Pot-cheese. Saltine crackers.
Watercress or celery.

Fruit dumplings (baked).
Liquid and hard sauce.

Tea or coffee.
Mixed nuts and raisins.
Any preferred table water.
Claret or cider.

CELERY SOUP.

This soup is made from white stock of mutton, veal, or chicken. The long stringy ends from loin of lamb or mutton chops can be used to advantage here, and four chops with the bones will generally yield sufficient for two people.

Free the meat from fat and chop fine in a chopping-bowl; it must be raw, and should measure a cupful. Dredge with a tablespoonful of flour, and put it into an agate-ware pot having a close-fitting cover.

Add the bones, pour over a pint of cold water, and let it soak an hour or longer before putting on to cook.

Heat gradually, and let simmer, closely covered, for several hours. When done, the bones will drop apart, and the meat will slip from them.

Now add a cupful of celery stalks and roots, chopped fine, and a tablespoonful of onion juice, and cook an hour or a little less; strain through a soup-strainer, add three tablespoonfuls sweet cream, boil up, salt and pepper to taste, and serve in cups. Pass the salted crackers known as "Banquets." There should be, when the soup is done, three fourths of a pint; if cooked so fast as to cook away, add a little boiling water. Use milk in the absence of cream, and thicken with a teaspoonful of flour blended with the same quantity of butter.

This substitute does not equal rich cream, but it will serve if necessary.

LAMB CHOPS (BROILED).

Order four fine lamb chops from the loin, lay them on a meat-board, and with a small, sharp knife cut out the bone from each one, careful not to spoil the shape of the chops.

Cut away carefully the long stringy ends, but leave the border of fat and the outer pink skin intact. Scrape from the bone the tiny roll of marrow, put it in the chop, press together gently, and wrap the long strip of fat around the whole, pinning securely with a small wooden skewer or a long clinch-nail.

You now have a round, compact chop, encircled with a border of delicious fat. The ends and bones are to be used for celery soup.

If but two chops are required for dinner, the others may be kept in the ice-chest and served, with a slice of lemon, for next morning's breakfast.

In broiling, observe the directions with the rule for serving porter-house steak.

Chops an inch in thickness will take about ten minutes to cook.

Count one hundred and fifty, turn; then count the same number for the other side. Now count ten, turn, and keep on in this way until four hundred has been counted.

Test by cutting into one of the chops, and if the meat looks red and raw return to the fire for a few more turns, counting five between each turn.

This constant turning prevents burning and over-cooking.

Take out the skewers, and put the chops on

warm, but not hot, plates, with a piece of butter, salt, and a spring of parsley or cress on each.

Broiled meats must be served immediately to be at their best.

BAKED POTATOES.

Select six potatoes, all of one size and as free from blemishes as possible.

Wash thoroughly in several waters, cut a small strip of skin from each end, and bake in a hot oven from thirty to sixty minutes.

The time required depends upon the size, age, and quality of the potatoes and the heat of the oven. Test occasionally with a fork, and when done puncture them all over to enable the steam to escape: this makes them light and mealy.

Keep hot in the open oven, uncovered, until ready to serve.

Peel those which are left over, slice, and warm up with white sauce for another meal.

LEMON MARMALADE.

Put the rind of a lemon on the stove to boil for half an hour in a pint of cold water. Drain (throw away the water) and chop very fine, adding also the lemon pulp, which should be freed from seeds, and a cupful of fresh water. Return to the fire and cook gently until the rind is very soft, about an hour : add a cupful of sugar and cook fifteen or twenty minutes longer, stirring occasionally to prevent burning. When skimming take off only the fine yellow froth gathered in little patches here and there.

When cool, put in a glass dish for the table.

This marmalade may be boiled down very thick, when it will keep in a dry place for months. Put in tumblers with brandied paper over the top the same as jellies.

SALTED ALMONDS.

These may be purchased at the confectioner's but can easily be done at home by any one with sufficient leisure.

Blanch the almonds by pouring boiling water over them ; the skins will slip off readily in a few minutes.

Then coat them with melted butter or olive-oil—a teaspoonful of oil to a cupful of nuts will be about right; spread on an agate-ware dish and brown in a hot oven.

They will need close watching and stirring to prevent burning. Sprinkle with salt while roasting.

Salted almonds are passed between the courses as an appetizer.

POT-CHEESE WITH WATERCRESSES.

Take half a cupful of fine fresh pot-cheese, add salt to taste, and as much sweet butter and cream as will be needed to make a soft, pliable mass; butter size of an egg will generally be enough. Work this together with a four-tined fork and afterwards with a broad-bladed knife until thoroughly incorporated, then smooth into a round mound, and garnish with watercresses.

Do not add the cream until the butter and cheese are thoroughly mixed together.

Pass saltine crackers.

If this is made a separate course, use little cheese-plates, and pass any candied fruit preferred, cherries or plums, ginger or pineapple.

FRUIT DUMPLINGS (BAKED).

Rub together a heaping dessert-spoonful of sweet butter with an even half-cupful of flour sifted with half a teaspoonful of baking-powder and one third of a teaspoonful of salt. Add three even tablespoonfuls of cold water and mix lightly with a spoon. Divide into halves, form each in a ball, lay on a floured board, and roll out lightly and quickly to the size of a large saucer. Put into the middle of each round, half of a fine winter greening (sliced), add a tablespoonful of sugar, a dust of flour, and a small lump of butter, and bring the paste up to the top and pinch it into ball shape, leaving a half-inch opening at the top for the steam to escape.

Bake in deep saucers, well buttered, for half an hour in a hot oven. Serve hot with sauce made of one even tablespoonful of flour with two tablespoonfuls of sugar and one tablespoonful of butter. Add a pinch of salt, stir until creamy, and then add a cupful of boiling water. Cook several minutes, and just before serving add flavoring of vanilla, wine, or brandy.

For the hard sauce, cream a dessert-spoonful of butter, add two thirds of a cup of confectioner's sugar, and a teaspoonful of water if necessary to make it soft and creamy. Stir at least ten minutes and grate nutmeg over it.

Peaches, fresh or canned, or cherries, pitted, may be substituted for the apples, if preferred.

XIII.

Tomato cream purée.

Pork chops or tenderloin.   Cream gravy.
Browned sweet potatoes, or turnips browned in butter.
Hot apple sauce.
Bread and butter.
Celery.   Water crackers.   Cheese.
Preserved citron.
Tapioca meringue.
Tea or coffee.   Salted almonds.

TOMATO CREAM PURÉE.

Fry a slice of salt pork, half an inch thick, until brown and put it, without the grease, into a saucepan with one cupful of tomatoes; boil gently half an hour, then strain through a coarse sieve and put back upon the stove while the dumplings are being prepared, thus:

Rub together half a teaspoonful of butter with two rounded tablespoonfuls of prepared flour, add a pinch of salt, and mix with the yolk of one egg beaten with a tablespoonful of milk. Mould into ten flat cakes, put them into the boiling tomatoes, cover, and cook two minutes; then add a cupful of rich, creamy milk in which has been boiled a teaspoonful of butter mixed with a teaspoonful of flour, and a piece of soda the size of a pea.

Take from the fire immediately, season to taste, and serve.

PORK TENDERLOIN OR FRIED PORK CHOPS. (TWO RIBS OF FRESH PORK.)

Have the chops cut from the prime part of the meat about an inch in thickness. Heat a spider smoking hot so as to brown the chops instantly when they go in.

Cover and fry rapidly for a minute, turn and fry the other side, then remove to a cooler part of the stove and cook each side ten minutes.

Pork should always be cooked slowly and thoroughly.

Put the chops on a platter, season, and set in the oven to keep hot.

Put a level teaspoonful of flour into the spider with a salt-spoonful of salt and a dust of pepper, stir the grease and brown sediment well into the flour, cook a moment, and add half a cupful of good, rich milk; stir till it is a smooth, creamy gravy and pour over the chops.

Pork tenderloins should be cut in pieces of uniform size, and a quarter of a pound of fresh fat pork should be allowed for each one. Make gravy as directed for the chops.

APPLE SAUCE (HOT).

Pare, quarter, and core four medium-sized Rhode Island Greening or Baldwin apples, put them in an earthen or agate dish with a close cover, pour on six tablespoonfuls of boiling water and six tablespoonfuls of granulated sugar. Cook rapidly ten minutes, then remove to a part of the stove where they will cook gently for an hour. Do not stir, and keep constantly covered. Be careful not to burn, but if they color a fine golden brown the flavor will be improved.

SWEET POTATOES BROWNED IN THE OVEN.

Wash two medium-sized sweet potatoes and cook either in boiling water or steam in a steamer; time from twenty to forty minutes.

Scrape off the skins with a knife, holding the potatoes in a napkin during the process.

Slice once lengthwise, sprinkle with sugar and a little butter, and brown in a quick oven.

Salt and pepper to taste.

TURNIPS BROWNED IN BUTTER.

Slice very thin two boiled white turnips, and dust them with flour, salt, and pepper.

Heat a tablespoonful of butter and one of milk, and fry the slices in this until a delicate brown. Only a moderate heat is required, as butter burns quickly.

The milk produces a fine crust.

TAPIOCA MERINGUE.

Scald a pint of rich fresh milk, and when cold soak a half-cupful of flake tapioca in it over night; in warm weather keep it in the refrigerator.

The next morning add the yolks of two eggs beaten with one heaping tablespoonful of granulated sugar, half a teaspoonful of salt, and the grated rind of nearly half a lemon. Bake half an hour in a moderate oven in a deep dish.

Whisk the whites of the eggs to a froth, add the juice of half of the lemon and two thirds of a cupful of sugar, spread over the top of the pudding, and brown a few minutes in the oven.

Serve cold.

XIV.

Ox-tail soup.

Roast veal, stuffed.

Rice croquettes.   Mashed squash.

or

Boiled onions.   Drawn butter.

Rhubarb sauce (cold).

Bread and butter.

Asparagus on toast.

Wine jelly.   Macaroons.

Tea or coffee.

Crystallized fruit.

OX-TAIL SOUP.

Order a fresh ox-tail jointed.

Wash in cold water and put it into a porcelain or agate kettle.

Pour on five quarts of cold water and after soaking for two hours bring gradually to a boil and simmer until the meat drops from the bones. Add a chopped carrot, a leek, several stalks of celery, some parsley, and a cupful of tomatoes. When these are soft, strain the soup and set it away to get cold: there should be a quart. Next day skim off the fat, put the soup over the fire, and, when hot, add a teaspoonful of salt, a tablespoonful of browned flour, half a teaspoonful of mixed spices (cloves, allspice, cinnamon, and nutmeg), a pinch of cayenne, and half a teaspoonful of sugar.

Sealed up hot in a glass preserving-jar, this soup will keep for two weeks in cold weather.

Use one cupful for two people, and add a few spoonfuls of water when re-heating it.

ROAST VEAL, STUFFED.

Cut the edges of a veal cutlet (to prevent curling) weighing about a pound and a half.

Pepper lightly and sprinkle over it about a quarter of a teaspoonful of thyme. Dredge with flour, put a bread-and-butter stuffing on one half, fold the other half over it, and lay the veal on a thin slice of fresh fat pork, on a deep earthen dish, cover tightly, and bake in a moderate oven for two hours.

Remove the veal to another dish, sprinkle with salt and browned bread crumbs, and return to the oven for a few minutes.

Add a little flour and water to the sediment in the baking-dish, salt to taste, boil up, and pour around the veal.

STEWED RHUBARB.

Make a syrup of one and a half cupfuls of

boiling water and one heaping cup of sugar: boil for a few minutes and add three cupfuls of rhubarb, skinned and cut into inch pieces. Do not skim the rhubarb, as much of the richness is lost in this way.

Stir for a minute, cover closely, and do not stir again. Simmer for fifteen minutes, and when cold pour carefully, so as not to break the pieces, into a dish for the table.

Each piece should lie by itself, surrounded by the rich syrup.

Rhubarb becomes very acid late in the season, when it would be well to make an extra quantity of syrup, which might be passed when serving the dish. One cup of sugar to half a cup of water is right proportion for the syrup.

RICE CROQUETTES.

Boil for half an hour, in a covered saucepan, a scant half-cupful of rice in one pint of boiling water, with half a teaspoonful of salt.

Make into oblong rolls the size of a hen's egg before the rice becomes entirely cold, and set away. When cold, dip each into a batter made of an egg beaten with a tablespoonful of flour, one of melted butter, and one of milk. Fry in a tablespoonful of salt-pork drippings or butter, turning frequently so that all sides will be delicately browned.

Some cooks prefer deep fat for frying croquettes. In this case, use a frying-basket, see that the fat is smoking hot, and lay the croquettes, when done, on brown paper, or, better still, on a piece of soft linen. Old table-linen when good for nothing else is of use here, but it must be kept scrupulously clean.

MASHED SQUASH.

Cut from a fine Hubbard squash enough to fill a pint bowl heaping full. Remove the seeds and soft part, peel, and cook in a steamer until very tender.

Mash fine, stir in one fourth of a teaspoonful of salt and one of butter, heap smoothly in a vegetable dish, pepper lightly, and put in the centre a lump of butter the size of an English walnut.

If summer squash is used, steam whole and mash seeds and skin.

BOILED ONIONS.

Peel and boil in boiling salted water, four medium-sized white onions; time, about thirty-five to forty minutes.

Take out with a skimmer, drain, and pour over them a sauce made in this way:

Stir to a cream a dessert-spoonful of butter, add one of flour, one third of a teaspoonful of salt, and, slowly, one third of a cupful of boiling milk, stirring constantly until smooth: cook a few minutes.

If preferred, the onions may be served with a simple dressing of salt and pepper, with a small lump of butter in each onion.

ASPARAGUS ON TOAST.

Get large-sized white asparagus; Oyster Bay is considered fine.

Remove the string, put in a pan of cold water, and rinse well to get out the grit. Tie together loosely with a broad band of muslin (or lay in the frame of an asparagus boiler) so that it may be lifted out easily when done. Pour on about a quart of boiling water with half a teaspoonful of salt, and cook gently, but steadily, for twenty minutes. Reserve, when done, a dozen stalks for next day's salad.

Lay the asparagus on a platter with the heads on two slices of well-toasted bread which have been slightly moistened with asparagus water. Make a sauce of one dessert-spoonful of butter, one of flour, a pinch of salt, dust of pepper, and one third of a cupful of the water the asparagus boiled in : cook a few minutes and pour over.

Serve as a separate course in place of a salad.

WINE JELLY.

Soak for ten minutes, four rounded teaspoonfuls of gelatine in two tablespoonfuls of cold water. Add a pinch of cinnamon, three heaping tablespoonfuls of granulated sugar, a few grains of salt, one even cup of boiling water, and stir well together. When cool, add five tablespoonfuls of sherry, cover closely to keep in the flavor of the wine, and set on ice to harden.

In hot weather use five teaspoonfuls of gelatine and make the day before it is wanted.

XV.

Boiled fish.
Hollandaise sauce.
Cucumbers or pickled cabbage.
Beef á la mode.
French fried potatoes.
Succotash.   Preserved grapes.
Lettuce
or
Apple salad.
Crackers.   Cheese.
Prune pudding.
Tea or coffee.   Nuts.
Crystallized ginger.

BOILED FISH.

Wash the fish quickly in cold water and wipe dry.

Dredge lightly with flour and pepper, roll in a napkin, place in a quart of boiling water to which has been added a little salt and a spoonful of vinegar, and cook, allowing about ten mintues to the pound for fresh fish. Salt, and serve on a platter garnished with parsley.

Any fish which remains may be made into a salad or into cakes and warmed in a steamer for next day.

HOLLANDAISE SAUCE.

Put into a saucepan which fits into the tea-kettle, a tablespoonful of butter; whip into it the yolk of an egg, add a pinch of salt and cayenne, two tablespoonfuls of boiling water, and a teaspoonful of cider vinegar.

Cook and stir until it is a little thick.

A few drops of lemon juice may be added. See that it is very hot, and keep the vessel covered to prevent a crust forming.

Serve a portion with each plate of fish.

BEEF À LA MODE.
(Top sirloin, one pound.)

Dredge a pound of top sirloin with a tablespoonful of flour and a dust of pepper, roll up, and put in a pot with a cupful of tomatoes. Add a tablespoonful of chopped salt pork (fried to extract the grease), pepper, dredge again with flour, cover closely, and bake four hours in a slow oven.

Serve the meat on a deep platter and pour the gravy (salted) over it.

The "Universal Pot" is best for this dish.

FRENCH FRIED POTATOES.

Wash and peel three potatoes, each the size of an egg, quarter them lengthwise, soak in cold water a few minutes, wipe dry, and fry in hot lard in a frying-basket.

Salt and pepper and serve hot.

If preferred the potatoes may be fried in a spider in a spoonful of hot pork drippings: keep the cover on until they are done, turning as the underside becomes brown.

Then remove the cover and allow them to get crisp. Serve at once.

SUCCOTASH.

A half-cupful of corn, either grated or canned, a half-cupful of cooked beans, salt and pepper to taste, and enough milk to make it a little juicy: add also a teaspoonful of flour and a heaping tablespoonful of butter. Stir, boil up and serve; long cooking toughens corn.

If string-beans are used, cut them into inch pieces and cook until tender in just enough salted water to cover: if lima beans, cook these also until done, or if they have been dried, soak twenty-four hours in cold water and then cook before adding.

APPLE SALAD.

Chop fine or slice in very thin slices a juicy Greening or Baldwin apple.

Add an equal amount of crisp white celery, a pinch each of salt and mustard and pepper, and finally two tablespoonfuls of cider vinegar. Stir and cover closely in a cold place for half an hour.

A few minutes before serving pour over the following dressing :

Stir together the yolk of an egg, a pinch of salt, one of sugar, a dust of cayenne, and add, drop by drop, two spoonfuls of olive-oil or melted butter.

The bowl may be rubbed with a slice of onion if that flavor is liked.

PRUNE PUDDING.

Rinse one scant cupful of prunes in cold water, pour on them one cupful of boiling water, add a scant cupful of granulated sugar, the grated rind and juice of a quarter of a lemon, and cook gently four or five hours, covered closely, in an earthern dish.

About three hours before dinner, melt a rounded tablespoonful of sweet butter in a cup nearly full of lukewarm milk which has been scalded.

Add half a compressed yeast-cake, one tablespoonful of sugar, one level teaspoonful of salt, and when these are dissolved, a well-beaten egg.

Beat and add two cupfuls of flour, sifted before measuring.

Stir thoroughly and set to rise, covered, in a temperature of about 90 degrees.

At the expiration of an hour, stir, and pour one third of the batter over the prunes, which have been taken out of the syrup and placed close together in an earthen pudding-dish (they should be cooled).

Sprinkle over the top of the batter a tablespoonful of sugar and grate on a little lemon rind, cover closely with a high cover (to give room for the batter to rise), and set for another hour in a warm place (90 degrees).

Bake in a moderate oven twenty or twenty-five minutes, uncovered. Serve hot with a sauce made from the juice of the prunes as follows:

Mix together one dessert-spoonful of butter, one teaspoonful of flour, one tablespoonful of sugar, the juice of quarter a lemon, the juice from the prunes, and enough boiling water to make a cupful.

Boil and serve hot. Pour the remainder of the batter into patty-pans, let them rise, covered, the same as the pudding, and bake. Eat hot, in place of bread, for dinner.

XVI.

Consommé julienne.
Fresh fish (baked).
Potato cakes.   Hot slaw.
String- or butter-beans.
Bread and butter.   Cucumbers.
Chicken salad.
Crackers.   Cheese.
Apple, peach, or rhubarb pie.
Tea or coffee.   Crystallized pineapple.

Alternative : Fried oysters.   Suet pudding.
Oranges.

CONSOMMÉ JULIENNE.

Heat a pint of soup-stock and add to it half a cupful of spring vegetables, shredded fine ; cook until tender and serve.

FRESH SHAD, BLUEFISH OR MACKEREL, WHITEFISH, PIKE, BASS, ETC.

(One to two pounds, stuffed and baked.)

If small use the whole fish, but if a large one take only one side. After cleaning inside and out, immerse in cold water, wash thoroughly, but quickly to avoid losing the sweet flavor, wipe gently with a clean napkin, dredge all over with flour, dust with pepper and a teaspoonful of salt, and fill with a stuffing of bread crumbs, the rule for which is given in Roast Pork.

Place the fish in a pan just wide enough for it and if half a fish is used lay two thin slices of salt pork on top of the stuffing—if an entire fish, on top of the fish. Dredge with flour and bake in a hot oven one hour. Lift carefully, so as not to break, and serve on a platter. If preferred the head and tail may be cut off before cooking; some cooks prefer to send to table whole, but to do so one must be expert in dishing, as the fish breaks easily.

The remainder of the uncooked part may be broiled or fried for another meal, but it must be kept directly on ice, as it spoils quickly.

The sooner fish reaches the fire after being taken from the water the finer the flavor.

Cold fish makes an excellent salad.

POTATO CAKES.

Mince very fine in a chopping-bowl two cupfuls of cold boiled or baked potatoes; sprinkle with half a teaspoonful of salt and a teaspoonful of flour; mix thoroughly with the yolk of an egg and a teaspoonful of butter, and mold into four round flat cakes. If the potatoes are too mealy to knead easily, add enough milk to make them of proper consistency; the cakes should be so soft as barely to hold together before cooking.

Make a batter of one tablespoonful of melted butter, two tablespoonfuls of cold milk, and one tablespoonful of flour, in a saucer. Dip each cake in the batter, careful not to break, and fry a delicate brown in either a teaspoonful of hot butter or salt-pork drippings. If any batter is left, pour it over the cakes before turning to fry on other side.

Use a pancake-turner.

Garnish with parsley.

HOT SLAW.

Put into a saucepan a quart of finely shredded cabbage; sprinkle with half a teaspoonful of salt, pour on a cupful of boiling water, cover, and cook half an hour. At the end of this time add half a cup of milk and a teaspoonful of butter, and cook down quite dry. Serve in a vegetable-dish with the following sauce: Beat an egg until frothy, add a tablespoonful of cider vinegar in which have been dissolved a pinch each of red pepper, mustard, salt, and sugar. Add a teaspoonful of butter, and set over a tea-kettle until a little thick, then add a quarter of a cup of boiling milk.

Stir, and serve.

STRING-BEANS.

Wash and pull the strings from a quart of fresh brittle string-beans ; break into inch pieces. If they do not snap easily they are old and will prove neither tender nor delicious. Cook for two hours in one pint of boiling water with half a teaspoonful of salt and a thin slice of fried salt pork without the grease.

Throw away the pork at the end of two hours, add to the beans a heaping tablespoonful of butter, a tablespoonful of flour, and plenty of pepper, cook up, and serve in a vegetable-tureen.

BUTTER-BEANS.

These are string-beans of a bright yellow color which will require only half as long time to cook as the green variety. Cook until tender in enough boiling salted water to cover.

Add a tablespoonful each of butter and flour, and cook down to a rich sauce.

A quart is enough for two meals, and they will be just as good warmed over.

Do not use pork with the butter-bean.

CUCUMBERS.

Peel a fresh, crisp cucumber, slice as thin as a knife blade and lay in strongly salted ice-water in the refrigerator for several hours.

Drain and serve (in a dish rubbed with an onion) with cayenne pepper, oil, and vinegar. The hot slaw should be omitted if cucumbers are served.

CHICKEN SALAD.

Place the body of a chicken, with the giblets, in a kettle, dredge with two teaspoonfuls of flour, pour on one cupful of boiling water, cover, and cook until the meat is so tender that it will break easily when twisted gently with a fork.

Cook so slowly and cover so closely that there need be no renewing of the water.

When done, take a cupful of the meat freed from bone and skin, cut (do not chop) into half-inch bits. Mash the liver with a knife-blade and stir it into the gravy. Take a tablespoonful of the gravy prepared in this way and stir it in with the cupful of chicken, add salt and pepper and, when cold, a cupful of celery, salted, peppered, and cut into half-inch pieces. Cover and put away in a cold place. Only the finest and whitest celery is fit to use for chicken salad. Just before sending to the table pour over the salad the following dressing. The quantity is sufficient for several salads and it will keep in a cold place for a week.

The cream may be sweet or sour, and if it will not whip readily, use it plain.

CREAM DRESSING.

In an agate-ware saucepan that fits over the teakettle, beat the yolk of one egg with half an even teaspoonful of salt, same of sugar, a pinch of cayenne, and half an even teaspoonful of flour.

Mix in a cup one tablespoonful of cider vinegar and half a teaspoonful of mustard, and add to the mixture in the saucepan. Stir well and add two tablespoonfuls of milk; cook over the teakettle for two minutes, stirring constantly from the bottom and sides. Remove from the fire and whip until cold, with a fork; then add four tablespoonfuls of cream, whipped to a stiff froth, and from three to eight tablespoonfuls of olive-oil.

If it should separate, warm it slightly by setting the bowl in warm water for a minute, and beat thoroughly.

PIE-CRUST (FLAKY).

Dip from the bag one even cupful of flour, add half a teaspoonful of salt, and sift two or three times.

With a knife cut into the flour half a cup of ice-cold lard to the size of peas, add four tablespoonfuls of ice-cold water, and stir with a spoon. If more water is needed, sprinkle in a few drops, but not as much as a tablespoonful.

Divide the paste in two equal parts, roll out one half and fit it into a pie pan.

Roll out the other half an eighth of an inch in thickness, dot it with a tablespoonful of sweet butter, dredge lightly with flour, fold up to the smallest compass possible, beat with the rolling-pin, and roll out once, pressing the rolling-pin this way and that during the process.

Slash with a knife in any desired pattern, lay upon the fruit in the pan, which contains the under crust, and pinch the edges together; then trim and bind the edges with a strip of muslin two inches wide, wet in cold water: this will keep in the juices. Bake at once in a hot oven. The under crust may be baked first if preferred.

Prick it all over with a fork to prevent blistering.

Never handle pie-crust any more than is absolutely necessary; the quicker it is made, and the colder the materials, the better it will be when baked.

Use just enough flour to keep it from sticking to the board and rolling-pin, and see that the hands are cool.

Prepare the fruit before beginning the paste, and be particular to have lard and butter as cold as possible.

RHUBARB, PEACH, OR APPLE PIE.

Rhubarb pies need an upper and lower crust, but peach and apple pies are delicious if made in deep saucers with only a round of upper crust laid lightly on top of the fruit, and not pinched to the edge of the saucer.

Peel and cut the fruit in slices, fill the saucers, sprinkle with sugar (two tablespoonfuls for each greening apple, and more or less according to the sourness of peaches), dredge with flour, dust on nutmeg or cinnamon, and they are ready for the covers.

Peel and cut the pie-plant into inch pieces, add one cup of sugar to three heaping cupfuls of rhubarb and a tablespoonful of flour, mix together, and place on the pan with the under crust, cover and bind as directed, and bake. Some cooks prefer not to peel the pie-plant for pies; the flavor however is more delicate to peel.

If cherries are used do not stone them. If canned fruit, reserve the juice, boil it with sugar and a little flour, and pour it into the pie after baking.

Pies need plenty of sugar.

CANDIED PINEAPPLE.

Cover one pint of sliced pineapple with half a pint of granulated sugar, let it stand until the sugar is dissolved, then drain off the juice closely. Cook for a few minutes, add the pineapple, cook two minutes, spread on a platter, and keep either in the warming-oven or the sunshine for a day. Turn the pieces and let it stand for another day.

Put away in glass, covered, in a dry place.

FRIED OYSTERS.

(Twenty medium-sized oysters.)

Crush to a powder four milk or sea-foam crackers: mix thoroughly with a half-teaspoonful of salt, unless the oysters are of the salt variety, which may be ascertained by tasting the juice.

Roll each oyster in the cracker crumbs and fry to a delicate brown in hot butter.

A lump of butter the size of an egg will be required, putting on the second half when the oysters are turned. Fry quickly, as oysters toughen and deteriorate by long contact with heat, every instant counting after they are done.

Have the pan and half of the butter hot when the oysters go in, but do not cover.

As soon as they are browned, turn with a broad-bladed knife: avoid using a fork, as oysters should not be pierced.

Put in the other half of the butter and brown the other side of the oysters.

Pepper lightly and serve on a hot platter. The sooner oysters and clams are cooked after leaving the shell, the better.

If any juice is left, mix with rolled cracker and fry in butter.

SUET PUDDING.

Sift twice, one and a half cupfuls of flour with one teaspoonful of baking-powder, half a teaspoonful of salt, and a quarter of a teaspoonful each of cloves and cinnamon. Chop into this half a cupful of suet, add half a cupful of stoned raisins, and mix well with the flour.

Beat together half a cupful each of milk and molasses and stir with the other ingredients.

Steam in a steamer an hour and a half. The fire should be steady and the water boiling before the pudding is put together.

The fire should not get low nor the water stop boiling before it is done.

For the sauce, cream a lump of butter the size of an egg, add a scant cupful of sugar, a tablespoonful of flour, a pinch of salt, and, gradually, a generous half-cup of boiling water.

Cook a few minutes and flavor with a wineglass of wine or brandy.

XVII.

Cream of Asparagus.
Veal cutlet (breaded).
Potatoes browned in milk.
Spinach.   Egg sauce.
Bread and butter.   Grape jelly.
Sliced tomatoes.   French dressing.
American club-house cheese.
Saratoga chip crackers.

Cottage pudding.   Wine sauce.
Tea or coffee.
Bananas.   Bonbons.

CREAM OF ASPARAGUS SOUP.

Two thirds of a pint of water in which asparagus has boiled.

To this add three or four stalks of fresh asparagus and one dessert-spoonful of butter mixed with one teaspoonful of flour, and let it boil until the stalks are tender. Mash these through the soup, add a pinch of cayenne pepper, two tablespoonfuls of cream, and salt to taste;

strain and serve with any kind of delicate crackers. If preferred, instead of using water in which asparagus has been boiled, cut up half a dozen stalks, and cook until tender in a pint (scant) of water: mash, and proceed as directed.

VEAL CUTLET.

Get a slice from the thick part of the leg weighing about a pound and a half. Divide in two pieces, using but one for the present dinner: the butcher will keep the other in his ice-chest.

Lay the veal on a meat-block or old pie tin and pound with a hammer until it becomes a jelly, pushing it together here and there to keep it thick and in shape: cut the edges every half-inch to prevent curling. Roll lightly in fine cracker crumbs and put it in a spider where a dessert-spoonful of butter is frying. Put another spoonful of butter in dots over the meat, fry rapidly for a minute, careful not to burn the butter; then remove to a cooler part of the range and cook each side for twenty minutes: it should be a fine brown.

Put the cutlet on a heated platter, and salt and pepper lightly. Add to the pan a teaspoonful of flour, stir and pour on half a cupful of boiling water: cook, add salt, and pour over the meat. Garnish with slices of lemon and serve a slice with each plate.

,Fresh fat pork is very nice for frying veal in instead of butter. Cut it into bits and use two tablespoonfuls. Six oyster crackers are sufficient for the breading.

Pound and cut the second cutlet in the same way : dip into a batter made of one tablespoonful of flour, a heaping tablespoonful of butter, melted, and half of a beaten egg.

Fry slowly in a little butter and make the gravy as directed for the breaded cutlet, adding a teaspoonful of lemon juice.

Garnish with watercresses.

Any meat left may be used for a salad ; chop, mix with lettuce, and serve with salad dressing.

POTATOES BROWNED IN MILK.

Melt in a small spider a heaping teaspoonful of table butter ; take from the fire and add a large pinch of salt, one third of a cup of milk, and one teaspoonful of flour ; stir, and add two cupfuls of very thinly sliced cold baked or boiled potatoes.

Stir all together, dust with black pepper, cover, and cook without further stirring for about fifteen minutes.

Set the spider on a wet cloth for a few minutes to sweat, and turn out on a dish for serving. The bottom will be brown and richly glazed, and the upper portion will be creamy.

Serve bottom upward and be careful not to break.

SPINACH WITH EGG SAUCE.

Put a small measure of spinach (beet tops, or dandelions may be substituted) in a pan of cold water for several hours.

Pick over each leaf carefully, using the entire root of the beets and as much of the roots of the spinach as possible. Wash in several waters to get out all the sand; when perfectly clean there will not be any sand on the bottom of the pan.

Cook in one quart of boiling water, to which a teaspoonful of salt has been added, for twenty minutes.

Skim out the greens and heap in a mound on a vegetable dish; serve with the following sauce:

Mash fine the yolk of a hard-boiled egg with a tablespoonful of melted butter; add a large pinch of salt, one of cayenne and one of mustard.

Beat the whole of one raw egg with a tablespoonful of melted butter, or olive-oil, add two tablespoonfuls cider vinegar, add the other ingredients, also two tablespoonfuls of milk. Cook over the teakettle until it is a little thick, add the white of the hard-boiled egg, finely chopped, and pass with the spinach.

Greens may also be served with hard-boiled eggs, sliced, and with a French dressing of vinegar, salt, oil, and pepper.

SLICED TOMATOES.

Pare with a sharp knife, two medium-sized, ripe, sound tomatoes. Put them on ice to become very cold, and, when ready to serve, slice and arrange them on a salad dish. The dish may first be rubbed with a slice of raw onion, if that flavor is liked.

Serve with French dressing ladled from a gravy-boat.

COTTAGE PUDDING.

Cream with the hand one fourth of a cup of butter, add a half-cup of sugar and the yolk of one egg. When very light add half a cup of milk which is blood warm, then one cup of flour sifted four times with a rounded teaspoonful of baking-powder and one fourth of a teaspoonful of salt. Whisk the white of the egg to a stiff froth, stir the cake up again, and add the egg.

Bake in muffin-rings, filling them a little less than half full.

Use two of these little cakes for dinner.

They should be served with wine sauce, made as follows:

Mix one even teaspoonful of corn-starch with

an even teaspoonful of butter and one heaping tablespoonful of sugar, add half a cup of boiling water, half a teaspoonful of caramel, and a small pinch of salt, and boil, covered, for a few minutes.

When ready to serve add a tablespoonful of sherry.

Oranges may be cut up and placed around the base of these puddings.

The remainder of the cakes may be frosted with confectioner's sugar and a little lemon juice, with sufficient water to make it a pliable paste.

This batter makes a good layer cake : bake in three layers, in a quick oven.

For chocolate filling, melt one cake (square) of chocolate in a saucepan over the teakettle, add eight even tablespoonfuls of confectioner's sugar, and thin the mixture with four tablespoonfuls of cream : flavor with half a teaspoonful of vanilla extract.

For cream cake, beat one egg with a tablespoonful of sugar, a pinch of salt, half a teaspoonful of lemon extract, and add slowly half a cup of boiling milk in which a heaping teaspoonful of flour has been cooked. Boil over the teakettle a few minutes, stirring constantly. Mix the flour first with a spoonful of cold milk, then add to the boiling milk.

Spread on the cakes when cool : frost the top layer.

XVIII.

Vegetable soup.
Beefsteak pudding.
Browned potatoes.
Stewed tomatoes.
Bread and butter.
Onion salad.   French dressing.
Banquet crackers.   Old English cheese.
Floating island.
Wafers.
Tea or coffee.
Apples.   Assorted nuts.

VEGETABLE SOUP.

Blend a tablespoonful of butter with one teaspoonful of flour, and pour on it, stirring constantly, three cupfuls of boiling water; cook for fifteen minutes, then add one and a half cupfuls of onion, turnip, and carrot, cut in quarters, salt to taste, a pinch of cayenne, and boil half an hour. At the end of this time skim out the vegetables, add to the soup two tablespoonfuls of tomatoes, and boil fifteen or twenty minutes.

Strain, and serve with minced parsley stirred through it.

Small oyster-crackers or Saratoga chips may be passed with this soup.

Serve the vegetables the following day warmed up in a cream sauce.

BEEFSTEAK PUDDING.

Put into the bottom of a quart earthen bowl two slices of salt pork which have been fried a delicate brown, but do not use the grease which tried out in the frying.

Place upon the pork one pound of raw round steak (freed from fat), and upon the steak a lump of butter the size of an egg; dust on black pepper, cover the bowl, and set in a pot with boiling water reaching half-way up the sides of the bowl.

Put a wire tea-stand, or meat-rack, in the bottom of the pot for the bowl to rest on, cover closely, and boil three hours, replenishing the the water as it cooks away from the boiling teakettle.

At the end of two and a quarter hours pour off half of the gravy, salt the meat with one third of a teaspoonful of salt, and lay over it a crust made in the following way:

Put one fourth of a cup of finely chopped suet into the chopping-bowl, add half a cup of flour in which has been sifted one half of a rounded teaspoonful of baking-powder and half of an even teaspoonful of salt; chop flour and suet together, and mix in with a spoon three tablespoonfuls of ice-water. If more wetting is needed, sprinkle in a few more drops of water; it should be of the consistency of biscuit-dough.

See that the suet is ice cold, and do not handle the dough more than is absolutely necessary, but get it over the fire as soon as possible.

The bowl should be left uncovered, so that the steam may reach the crust, and the pot must be covered closely.

When done, pour out on a deep platter, meat-side down, and over all pour the gravy. This is made by cooking two lamb kidneys (chopped fine), with one slice of onion and a pinch of cayenne pepper, in a cup of cold water for thirty minutes. Cook gently, and take off the scum carefully as it rises, or the gravy will be strong and disagreeable. The little veins and fat in the centre of the kidneys should be removed, and they should be washed in cold water before being chopped.

Thicken the gravy with a tablespoonful of flour which has been mixed smooth with the gravy from the meat.

If too thick add a little boiling water.

This dish may be prepared on the previous day, and will be fully as delicious as when first cooked.

Warm over by setting the bowl containing it in a steamer over boiling water.

BROWNED POTATOES.

Wash and peel two medium-sized potatoes, split them, dust with salt, dredge lightly with flour, lay upon a baking-tin, closely covered, and bake in a hot oven. When soft, turn them, put a small lump of butter on each piece, dust with pepper, and brown a little longer, uncovered.

To be right they should have a crisp brown coat and be mealy inside.

The mealiness depends on the quality of the potatoes and the heat of the oven. A slow oven is not good.

STEWED TOMATOES.

Add to two cupfuls of tomatoes a scant half-teaspoonful of salt and a sprinkle of cayenne pepper, and stew gently for half an hour, stirring occasionally to prevent burning.

Add a pinch of sugar and a teaspoonful of butter, and cook for ten minutes longer with the saucepan covered.

Use agate or earthenware, as the acid of tomatoes corrodes tin.

ONION SALAD.

Slice a Bermuda or Spanish onion in wafer-like slices, and soak in enough cold salted water to cover, several hours. Drain, rinse in cold fresh water, and serve with a simple dressing of vinegar, pepper (black and cayenne) and salt, with oil in any desired proportion.

This is a most healthful salad, and it may be eaten with cold sliced potatoes and lettuce.

The silver-skinned, or white, onion, may be used if the others are out of market.

FLOATING ISLAND.

Mix half even teaspoonful of flour with one of cold milk, add two thirds of a cup of boiling milk, and place the vessel containing it in a saucepan of boiling water to cook, stirring occasionally, while whipping the white of an egg to a stiff froth.

Then beat to a cream the yolk of the egg with a heaping tablespoonful of granulated sugar and a pinch of salt. Pour the boiling milk upon the yolk and sugar, beat well and return to the saucepan, stirring continually while cooking two minutes.

Remove from fire and add half a teaspoonful of lemon extract (or other flavoring).

Add to the frothed white one teaspoonful of lemon juice, a few grains of salt, and a teaspoonful of confectiouer's sugar.

Whisk together and lay on top of the hot custard. Cover closely, and, when cold, pour into a glass dish for the table.

Serve ice cold.

Strawberries, or ripe peaches (cut up), may be served with this dish if liked.

Pass almond or vanilla wafers.

VANILLA WAFERS.

One fourth of a cup of butter, one cup of flour lightly put in, one rounded teaspoonful of baking-powder, one fourth of a teaspoonful of salt, one yolk of egg, one half-cup of moist sugar, three tablespoonfuls of cold water, one scant teaspoonful of flavoring.

Sift flour, baking-powder, and salt four times, and rub in the butter.

Beat the yolk and sugar to a cream, add flavoring, and, by the spoonful, the water.

Then add this to the flour, stirring it in with the hand till the mass is light and smooth. Keep the fingers spread apart while beating.

Put this mixture in half-teaspoonfuls on the inverted bottoms of well-buttered pans, at intervals of two inches. Spread a little by a circular motion of the spoon tip, and bake in a quick, but not fierce, oven a few minutes.

XIX.

Oyster soup.
Pork and beans.
Spiced tomato sauce (hot).
Hot corn bread.   Cider.
Salted almonds.
Celery.   Cream cheese.   Crackers.
Preserved ginger.
Indian pudding.
Tea or coffee.
Nut candies.   Apples.

OYSTER STEW.

(Twenty-five freshened oysters.)

See the oysters opened and if possible get those which have been "freshened," as they are preferable to the salt ones. Put a pint of rich sweet milk on the fire to scald, and in another saucepan the strained oyster liquor: skim the latter well as it boils. Add to it a lump of butter the size of an egg, blended with a half-teaspoonful of flour (not more), and when this is cooked, add the oysters and set the saucepan where the contents will keep at the boiling-point for a minute or two. Then add the scalding milk and serve at once. Add salt and pepper to taste, with a few drops of onion juice.

Do not allow the stew even to boil up or simmer after the milk goes in, or it will be sure to curdle. Serve with oyster-crackers or small squares of toasted bread.

PORK AND BEANS.

Pick over and wash one pint of pea-beans and soak over night in a pint of cold water. In the morning add two more cups of water and cook for ten minutes. At the expiration of this time stir in a half-teaspoonful of baking-soda and skim off the froth. Drain off all the water and put the beans in a pot with a fitted cover: a pipkin or agate-ware vessel will do if a regular bean-pot is not at hand.

Mix a pint of fresh boiling water with half a teaspoonful of salt, a pinch of cayenne, and an even tablespoonful of either sugar or molasses. Pour this over the beans, set in a moderate oven, and bake slowly for three hours, covered: at the end of this time add half a pound of washed salt pork (score the rind every half inch), and press it down so that the top comes even with the top of the beans, and dust with black pepper.

If the water has cooked away, add a little from boiling teakettle, just enough to cover. Bake another hour, uncovered, then cover closely and cook until night, but do not add any more water.

Beans should cook continuously in a slow oven from ten in the morning until six at night: if cooked fast they will be too dry.

When done, to be just right, the juice should show itself when the pot is tilted half-way up. The pork rind should be almost like jelly, and slightly browned, and every bean should be whole but soft.

Serve in a deep dish and put the pork on a platter garnished with any seasonable greens.

SPICED TOMATO SAUCE (HOT).

Melt a lump of butter the size of a large nutmeg, and pour in one cupful of tomatoes, either fresh or canned. Add salt to taste; a pinch of cayenne, a slice of onion, a dust of flour, and a pinch of ground cloves and cinnamon. Stew gently one hour, stirring often to prevent burning, and keep the saucepan covered.

Strain through a sieve which will keep back the seeds, and add a teaspoonful of vinegar if liked.

This sauce is delicious poured over hashed meats which are served on toast.

CORN BREAD.

Half an even cup of Graham flour, half an even cup of yellow corn-meal sifted, with one teaspoonful of baking-powder, half a teaspoonful of salt, and one teaspoonful of sugar. Add half a cup of suet and chop all together. Add one well-beaten egg, and one full cup of cold water; beat the egg in the water.

Pour into a greased pan or pudding-mould, set in a steamer, and steam one hour; then bake in the oven half an hour.

Half a pint of loppered milk may be used instead of the water, in which case half a level teaspoonful of baking-soda should take the place of the baking-powder; this should be well beaten into the milk.

Sour milk makes a much better corn bread than water, and may easily be secured by a little planning beforehand.

INDIAN PUDDING.

Heat one cup of milk, add two rounded tablespoonfuls of yellow corn-meal, stir, and boil for three minutes, take from the fire, add one teaspoonful of butter, one tablespoonful of New Orleans molasses, one cup of cold milk, one well-beaten egg, a half-teaspoonful of ground ginger, a pinch of cloves and cinnamon, and a quarter of a teaspoonful of salt.

Bake in a very slow oven two hours.

To be right, the pudding should be like a solid custard floating in whey.

Serve with a sauce of powdered sugar, three spoonfuls, stirred to a cream with one of creamed butter.

XX.

Oysters on the half-shell.
Banquet-crackers.
Roast pork.
Boiled hominy.
Baked apple-sauce.
Bread and butter. Celery.
Grapefruit.
Chocolate pudding with Sea-foam cream.
Tea or coffee.
Bonbons.

ROAST RIB AND LOIN OF PORK.
(THREE POUNDS.)

Always buy young pork, as it is sweeter and more tender.

Put meat on a rack in a roasting-pot; an agate kettle with a close-fitting cover will answer.

Dredge the pork liberally with flour, pour over a scant pint of boiling water, cover, and cook slowly an hour and a half.

Take up the meat and put it in a dripping-pan, ribs upward, and lay on it a stuffing made of one quart of stale bread crumbs steamed moist in a cup of water, and mixed thoroughly with a salt-spoon of salt, a half-teaspoonful of black pepper, and a dessert-spoonful of butter.

Roast one hour in a hot oven, basting occasionally with the gravy in the roasting-pot (from which all grease has been skimmed.)

Keep the gravy hot. Serve the meat on a platter garnished with any seasonable green. Thicken the gravy with one dessert-spoonful of flour blended with two of cold water, add salt to taste, a dust of cayenne, boil up, and serve.

The second day the pork may be sliced and served cold with fried hominy.

A succeeding meal may be prepared in this way:

Free it from all fat and mince one cupful and warm up in a sauce made of a dessert-spoonful of butter, one of browned flour, and half a cup of boiling water, with salt and pepper. Serve on stale bread, toasted and dipped in salted boiling water. Butter the toast slightly after it is moistened.

BOILED HOMINY.

Put one cupful of hominy into three cupfuls of boiling water; add half a teaspoonful of salt, stir until the hominy boils, then set on back of stove, closely covered, to simmer four or five hours: stir occasionally. Use the Universal pot, or an earthen one set upon a stand, so that the hominy will not burn.

A double boiler is not so good, as hominy needs a closer action of the fire than it can get through water.

BAKED-APPLE SAUCE.

Peel, quarter, and core four Rhode Island Greening apples. Put them in an agate or earthern dish with four tablespoonfuls of granulated sugar and four of boiling water.

Cover closely and bake in a moderate oven from one half to three quarters of an hour.

If desired hot, dot the apples with small pieces of butter just before taking from the oven, leave the cover off, and bake a little longer. Serve in the baking-dish, with a napkin pinned around it. If to be served cold, pour carefully, when cool, into a glass dish, but do not break the fruit, as the pieces should retain their shape.

CHOCOLATE JELLY.

Mix two even teaspoonfuls of cocoa with one heaping tablespoonful of granulated sugar, and pour on slowly, stirring constantly, one cupful of boiling water. Boil one minute, and add four even teaspoonfuls of corn-starch mixed with one teaspoonful of cold water, and one tablespoonful of rich cream and a pinch of salt. Boil and stir for seven or eight minutes.

Take from the fire and add half a teaspoonful of extract of vanilla : pour into a shallow dish, and when cold spread Sea-foam cream on top.

Serve ice cold.

XXI.

Broth.

Lamb (browned in spiced sauce.)
Saratoga potatoes. Onions.
Dinner rolls. Lemon marmalade.

Potato salad.
Cream cheese. Biscuits.
Tapioca cream.
Tea or coffee. Fruit.

LAMB BROWNED IN SPICED SAUCE.

Get a shank of mutton weighing about a pound. Trim off the dried outer skin, wipe carefully with a damp cloth, dredge all parts plentifully with flour, and dust with black pepper.

Lay the meat in an agate kettle, add a tiny piece of bay leaf, one clove, a pinch of cayenne, one thin slice of onion, and an inch piece of cinnamon stick, pour on a full cup of boiling water, and cook gently two hours, being careful that it does not burn. The water should all be cooked away by this time, only a spoonful or two of rich brown gravy remaining, and the meat should slip easily from the bones.

Transfer the meat (do not use the bones) to a deep platter.

Season with salt, and pour over a gravy made from the sediment in the baking-pan: a spoonful of wine or lemon juice may be added to this if desired.

Pour into the pot in which the meat was cooked, a cupful and a half of boiling water, add the water which was drained from the onions, and cook gently ten or fifteen minutes. Add a little salt and a few sprigs of parsley, boil up and strain; this makes the soup, and there should be about three fourths of a pint.

Serve a thin slice of lemon with each portion.

SARATOGA CHIPS.

Slice in wafer-like slices, two medium-sized potatoes and let them soak for half an hour in a quart of salted water.

Drain and dry with a cloth and fry in boiling-hot lard until they are a pale brown. Put in only a few at a time, and lay them when done on a sheet of brown paper, to absorb the grease; serve hot.

Saratoga potatoes may now be found at any first-class grocer's shop and these need only be warmed a few minutes in an open dish in the oven.

ONIONS BROWNED IN BUTTER.

Slice two cupfuls of onions, add one fourth of a teaspoonful of salt and one cupful of boiling water. Cook, covered, until tender, then drain off the water (reserve this for the soup-pot), add one even tablespoonful of butter, and stir well after the butter is melted, and fry until a delicate brown.

Do not stir again but move the spider about to prevent burning.

Keep onions in cold water while paring, to prevent the eyes from smarting.

POTATO SALAD.

Beat the yolk of an egg with half a level teaspoonful of flour, one third of a teaspoonful of salt, a pinch of sugar, and two pinches of cayenne pepper.

Add two tablespoonfuls of boiling water and cook over the teakettle, stirring constantly, two minutes.

Then remove, add one tablespoonful of cider vinegar, three tablespoonfuls of cream or milk, and either a tablespoonful of oil or melted butter with a few drops of onion juice. Beat well, and to two tablespoonfuls of this sauce add a half-cupful of mashed and seasoned potatoes.

Beat for several minutes, and heap on a mound of spinach which has been cooked, drained, and seasoned. Pour the remainder of sauce over all.

This may be eaten hot or cold. Watercresses, celery, or cabbage, or any salad greens may be substituted for the spinach.

RAISED BISCUIT OR DINNER ROLLS AND BREAD.

Two heaping cups of flour sifted three times. Put into an agate two-quart vessel having a fitted cover one even cupful of lukewarm water, a heaping teaspoonful of sweet butter, one even teaspoonful of salt and one of sugar.

Add to this one fourth of a cake of Fleischmann's compressed yeast, dissolved in one teaspoonful of the water.

Mix well and stir in the flour, using a stout spoon for the purpose and mixing thoroughly.

Cover closely and let rise about five hours. At the end of this time the dough should be light and soft and nearly fill the dish. Turn out on a lightly floured board or pie pan and knead a few minutes, using not more than a teaspoonful of flour for the entire kneading.

Put into a saucer another spoonful of flour, cut the dough into twenty pieces, roll each into a ball between the palms, dipping them in the flour in the saucer to prevent sticking.

Put them in a greased pan which is two inches deep, and do not let the rolls touch at any point. Cover closely with a high cover, or another pan, and let them rise about three hours.

They should by that time have become as one, with slight depressions showing the dividing line, and they should also be moist to the touch. Bake in a hot oven fifteen minutes, wrap in a hot napkin, and serve.

They may be heated for breakfast by putting them in the oven in a closely covered dish.

If wanted for six o'clock dinner, begin operations by nine in the morning.

The temperature for raising should be from 80° to 90°.

Never set sponge on a hot surface; the foundation on which the pans rest should only be blood-warm; the heat must come from radiation.

Too much heat from any source will cause sponge to become thin and pasty, and the dough will lose all its elasticity.

For bread, put into a three-quart basin two even cupfuls of lukewarm water, one heaping tablespoonful of sweet butter, one teaspoonful of sugar, and one heaping teaspoonful of salt.

Melt half a yeast-cake in a spoonful of the water, add, and stir until all has been dissolved; then stir in five cupfuls of flour, measured before sifting, and sifted three times. Stir very thoroughly, cover closely with a tin cover, and when the mass has risen to the top of the basin, turn on a lightly floured board and knead half an hour.

kneading in one scant half-cupful of flour. The dough should now be almost as elastic as a rubber ball.

Put it back in the basin, cover, and let rise to double its bulk or a little more. Then knead again a minute, using not more than a teaspoonful of flour.

Cut off four little pieces, roll into balls, set to rise again, and when they have trebled in size, set in a steamer for half an hour; they will keep several days in the bread-box and may be used for dumplings in meat stews.

Cut the remainder of the dough into loaves of any desired size, fill pans one third full, cover, and raise until they have doubled in bulk, when bake in a moderate oven.

Small individual loaves are best.

Temperature and time for raising are the same as for biscuit. Kneading should be done with the "heel of the palm."

TAPIOCA CREAM.

Soak three tablespoonfuls of flake tapioca over night in half a cup of cold water.

In the morning add one cup of rich milk and a large pinch of salt and cook half an hour in a double boiler, stirring frequently.

Beat the yolk of one egg with two tablespoonfuls of sugar, thin with a little of the hot milk, stir well, and add to the tapioca.

Whisk to a stiff froth the white of the egg, add this also, cook a minute, flavor with a half-teaspoonful of vanilla and a dust of nutmeg, and pour into a dish for the table.

Serve ice cold.

This dessert may be varied by adding to the top a few spoonfuls of whipped cream and serving with it a teaspoonful of grape jelly to each plate.

XXII.

Purée of beans.
Porter-house steak.
Potato croquettes.
Boiled beets.
Onions baked in milk.
Bread and butter.   Tomato marmalade.
Asparagus salad.
Crackers.   Cheese.
Chocolate pudding.
Tea or coffee.   Oranges.

PURÉE OF BEANS.

Soak over night a half-cupful of dried beans in a quart of cold water.

In the morning throw away the water, cover with a pint of fresh cold water, add a slice of lightly browned salt pork (but not the grease), a slice of onion, a quarter of a teaspoonful of salt, and cook until the beans are mushy. Strain, add to the liquor a half-teaspoonful of butter rubbed with the same of flour, boil up, and add enough boiling milk to make the soup of an agreeable consistency, with salt and pepper to taste.

POTATO CROQUETTES.

Mash two cupfuls of boiled potatoes and three tablespoonfuls of hot milk, in which is melted a tablespoonful of butter and a third of a teaspoonful of salt.

Whip to a cream with a fork, form into egg-shaped rolls, dip, when cold, into cracker-dust, then into beaten egg, and fry in a frying-basket in deep hot lard.

Try first a small piece of bread to ascertain the amount of heat. If too hot the croquettes will burn; if not hot enough they will soak fat, which renders them unfit to eat.

If preferred, they may be browned in a spoonful of butter.

BOILED BEETS.

Select three beets of equal size, wash carefully so as not to break the skins, and do not trim the stalks too closely, as they will bleed and lose their sweetness. Cook in a steamer, and when tender put into cold water long enough to enable you to slip the skins off.

Serve hot, sliced, with butter, pepper, and salt, or heat two tablespoonfuls of cider vinegar, add a tablespoonful of butter, with salt and pepper, and pour this dressing over them. Serve hot.

While cooking, do not pierce the beets any oftener than is necessary ; the time for cooking will be from one to three hours, according to their age.

ONIONS BAKED IN MILK.

Peel and slice thin three cupfuls of white onions. Put in a deep earthen dish, dredge with a tablespoonful of flour and a little pepper, dot with a lump of butter the size of half an egg, and pour on a cupful of rich milk.

Bake in a good oven half an hour, sprinkle on a half-teaspoonful of salt, and serve in the baking-dish.

TOMATO MARMALADE.

One quart of ripe tomatoes, skinned and sliced. Put on the stove, with half a cupful of cider vinegar, one third of a cup of sugar, one teaspoonful of salt, one teaspoonful of mixed ground spices ; cook slowly, and stir often with a wooden spoon.

When reduced to a little less than one half, it is done.

Put away in tumblers covered with brandied paper. Canned tomatoes may be used, but are not so good.

ASPARAGUS SALAD.

Lay one dozen asparagus stalks, boiled in salted water, on a salad dish, and serve with a simple French dressing of vinegar, oil, salt, and pepper.

CHOCOLATE PUDDING.

Heat one and one quarter cups of rich milk with half a square of chocolate, stirring constantly until the chocolate is dissolved; then add two rounded tablespoonfuls of corn-starch mixed with a quarter of a cup of cold milk. Let this boil for ten minutes in a saucepan of boiling water; then add the yolk of an egg beaten with one tablespoonful of sugar and a pinch of salt.

Beat well, cook one minute, flavor with half a teaspoonful of vanilla, turn into a mould, and serve ice cold with the following sauce:

Froth the white of the egg, and whip it into half a cup of boiling milk, sweetened with a tablespoonful of sugar, add a few grains of salt, and flavor with half a teaspoonful of vanilla and a dust of nutmeg. Set on ice.

XXIII.

Clam chowder.
Salad of cold meat.
Cream cheese.   Crackers.
Blackberry pudding.
Tea or coffee.   Cream nut candies.

CLAM CHOWDER.
(One dozen clams.)

Peel and slice very thinly a cupful of raw potatoes; add a thinly sliced, medium-sized onion, and a cupful of boiling water, with a tablespoonful of fried salt pork (without the grease), and boil gently until the vegetables are tender; then add a half-cupful of stewed tomatoes.

When this boils, add the strained clam juice (there should be about a cupful), and skim, after boiling up. Now stir in a tablespoonful of butter, blended with half a teaspoonful of flour.

Boil a few minutes, and add the clams, chopped very fine in the chopping-bowl, or meat-grinder.

Allow the chowder to come quickly to a boil, and remove from the fire immediately.

Simmering or long boiling will make clams tough and indigestible. Pour into a hot tureen, and set in the oven until wanted.

COLD MEAT SALAD.

Any cold meat of the white kind, such as veal, lamb, or poultry; cut a cupful into small pieces without the fat, add salt and pepper, and mix with the same amount of celery, cut up, or watercresses.

Heap upon lettuce leaves; the large outside leaves will answer. Pour on a salad dressing of any preferred kind, and serve ice cold.

The crisp inner parts of white cabbage may be used if other greens are not obtainable.

The following dressing may be used:

SALAD DRESSING.

Stir the yolk of an egg with two tablespoonfuls of either olive-oil or melted butter; add one tablespoonful of vinegar in which has been dissolved a salt-spoonful of salt, a small pinch of cayenne, and a large pinch of mustard.

BLACKBERRY PUDDING.

Take half a cupful of flour and mix with it half a teaspoonful of baking-powder and a large pinch of salt. Sift several times. Cut into this, with a knife, an even dessert-spoonful of butter and add one fourth of a cup of milk. The mixture should be quite soft.

With a spoon spread it on the bottom of a baking-dish or cake-mold, cover the paste with a thick layer of blackberries, and steam half an hour in a steamer, or bake in the oven with a cover over the dish. Serve with sugar and cream, or with a creamy hard sauce.

Cherries or huckleberries, apples or peaches, may be used in the same way.

XXIV.

Clam soup.
Round steak with onions.
Yellow turnips and potatoes mashed together.
Baked Hubbard squash.
Celery.
Sweet-clover cheese.   Crackers.
Steamed pudding with oranges or canned or stewed fruit.
Tea or coffee.   Chocolate creams.

CLAM SOUP.

Drain the juice from a dozen clams and put it on the stove to scald. If soft-shell clams are used, first wash them thoroughly in their own liquor, with the addition of a half-cup of cold water, and strain through cheese-cloth. Chop the clams very fine and add to the juice when it reaches the boiling-point: boil up quickly *once* and immediately remove to a part of the stove where they will merely keep hot. The longer clams boil, the tougher and more indigestible they become. Do not even allow them to simmer after the first quick boil.

In another saucepan put two cupfuls of rich milk (skimmed milk will never produce the best results), and when it boils add a tablespoonful of butter blended with an even teaspoonful of flour, and a small pinch of cayenne pepper. Boil a moment and set where it will keep hot, but not cook.

When ready to serve, pour the clams into the milk, stir and serve immediately in hot soup plates with any preferred crackers.

BEEFSTEAK AND ONIONS (FRIED).

Round steak is usually preferred for this dish. Cut off a piece measuring about five inches square. Pound to a jelly with a hammer on a meat-block or old pie tin.

Slice four medium-sized onions after peeling, put them into a frying-pan with a cup of boiling water, and stew until the water is all gone; do not stir.

Then add a little salt and pepper, and a heaping tablespoonful of butter, and fry until the onions are a fine brown.

Fry the steak in a *hot* frying pan, and do not salt until it is on the platter. Then add salt and butter, pile the onions on top and serve immediately.

POTATOES AND TURNIPS MASHED TOGETHER.

Wash, peel, and slice in inch-thick slices, enough yellow (Rutabaga) turnips to fill a pint bowl. Cover with boiling water, and cook rapidly thirty or forty minutes. When tender, drain and mash fine; pass through the potato-press, or mash fine a pint bowl of hot boiled potatoes and add to the turnips, season with a teaspoonful of salt, beat well together and heap in a dish, smoothing the top over with a knife-blade.

Make a long deep trench, on top of which put a lump of butter the size of a small egg.

Set in a hot oven until wanted.

Next day, slice, dredge with flour, and fry in salt-pork drippings or butter.

BAKED SQUASH.

Cut a slice four inches thick from a fine Hubbard squash.

Remove the seeds, place on a baking-dish, cover closely, and bake in a hot oven for an hour, or until soft.

Then scrape squash from the rind, mash, season with a spoonful of butter, salt and pepper to taste, pile on a vegetable-dish, and keep hot in the oven until wanted; or send to the table on a platter, just as it comes from the oven, in which case each person will season his own portion.

STEAMED PUDDING WITH ORANGES.

Sift three times, one even half-cupful of flour, with one half rounded teaspoonful of baking-powder and one third even teaspoonful of salt.

Cut into this one heaping teaspoonful of ice-cold butter with a knife. Add three heaping tablespoonfuls of cold milk, stir together lightly and quickly, using a spoon for the purpose, put into a buttered mold or bowl and set in a steamer for half on hour. When done, turn into a shallow pudding-dish and serve with the following sauce: Cook for ten minutes one half cupful of boiling water, a few grains of salt, and two heaping tablespoonfuls of granulated sugar. Then add a half-teaspoonful of corn-starch, wet with one spoonful of cold water, cook and add a teaspoonful of caramel and a fine orange which has been peeled and cut into pieces the size of nutmegs. When this is thoroughly hot, but not boiling, pour over the pudding.

Pass with this pudding, a hard sauce made of one tablespoonful of butter stirred to a cream, the half of a raw egg yolk, and half a cupful of confectioner's sugar, beaten together until very light. Flavor with a pinch of grated orange-rind.

If canned cherries or fruit are used instead of oranges, heat them for a few minutes and add more sugar to the juice.

Only the egg sauce will be needed with canned or stewed fruit.

AFTER-DINNER COFFEE.

Mix two dessert-spoonfuls of coffee ground moderately fine with a scant teaspoonful of raw egg and two dessert-spoonfuls of cold water.

Pour on this two thirds of a cup of boiling water, stir, cover closely, and let it boil up; then remove from the fire immediately.

Let it stand, to settle, a few minutes, and strain into a hot coffee-pot through a wet cheese-cloth laid on a wire strainer.

In this way the last drop of coffee will be perfectly clear.

XXV.

Raw oysters or clams.
Fresh ham. Savory stuffing.
Apple sauce (hot or cold).
Breaded turnips.
Baked sweet potatoes.
Green tomato chili sauce.
French bread. Butter.
Celery or any salad of the chicory family.
Roquefort cheese on brown-bread fingers.
Princess cream, or pineapple with floating island.
Wafers, or sponge cake.
Tea or coffee. California grapes.

Alternative: Roast duck. Onion stuffing.
Potato balls (baked).
Spiced peaches.
Corn-starch pudding, or chocolate jelly with custard.

FRESH HAM.

Order a small fresh *pig* ham. Have one third

of it sliced off from the large end for frying (this may be left in the butcher's ice-chest until needed); the remaining part should be boned and trimmed for roasting.

Put a quart of bread-crumbs a little stale in a bowl, pour over enough boiling water to make a pliable paste, stir in a tablespoonful of thyme, a teaspoonful of salt, a half-teaspoonful of black pepper, one pinch of red pepper, and a rounded dessert-spoonful of butter. Work this into a mass, and stuff the ham with it. Dredge thoroughly with flour, pepper liberally, and set on a meat-rack in a dripping-pan.

The oven should be quite hot for the first hour. At the end of this time pour a cup of boiling water in the pan, and moderate the fire. Bake three hours slowly.

Salt the meat, and if it is not brown, quicken the fire with kindlings, and set in the oven for fifteen minutes longer. Make the gravy by blending a tablespoonful of flour with two tablespoonfuls of cold water; pour in a cupful of boiling water and add to the dripping-pan. Salt to taste, boil up, skim off the fat and serve in a gravy-boat.

For succeeding meals serve the ham sliced cold with hot gravy.

BREADED TURNIPS.

Peel and boil until tender one large white

turnip. When cold, slice in four slices, bread with saltine cracker dust, and brown in a half-teaspoonful of butter in a frying-pan.

BAKED SWEET POTATOES.

Brush clean two or three sweet potatoes of one size, and bake in a moderate oven, from an hour to an hour and a half, according to the size of the potatoes and the heat of the oven. When done they should feel soft and yielding when pressed with the fingers. Try them occasionally while cooking with a fork.

Any that are left over may be peeled, sliced, and broiled; butter and salt them as soon as they leave the gridiron.

They may also be browned in the oven by brushing with butter and sprinkling with sugar.

GREEN TOMATO CHILI SAUCE.

One quart of sliced green tomatoes, one pint of sliced white onions, two chopped green peppers, one heaping tablespoonful of salt; mix all together and set away in an earthen dish overnight.

Next morning drain thoroughly, chop into peas, pour over one pint of cider vinegar, add one teaspoonful of mixed ground spice (cinnamon, cloves, allspice, and nutmeg), one tablespoonful of brown sugar, and cook slowly for twenty minutes.

Add a red-pepper pod to the sauce, and let it remain until peppery enough. Add more salt if needed. Keep in a cool place in a stone jar, tightly covered. A few mustard seeds may be added, also chopped celery and grated horse-radish if liked.

PRINCESS CREAM.

Soak for half an hour one rounded tablespoonful of gelatine and a pinch of salt in four tablespoonfuls of rich milk. Beat the yolk of one egg with two tablespoonfuls of granulated sugar and a tiny pinch of salt until creamy, and add one cupful of boiling milk.

Set this in another saucepan containing boiling water, and boil and stir four minutes.

Now add the gelatine, cook (stirring) for one minute, take from the fire, and whip in the white of the egg, which has been beaten to a stiff froth.

Flavor with three fourths of a teaspoonful of vanilla, or, if preferred, a little sherry.

Pour into a glass dish, and serve ice cold with cake or wafers.

Princess cream should be made the day before it is to be used, in summer, and kept on ice until wanted.

In cold weather it may be made in the morning if it is to be used at a late dinner.

Spread the Sea-foam cream over the top,

delicately flavored with caramel, wine, or coffee.

Serve with caramel cream sauce.

PINEAPPLE WITH FLOATING ISLAND.

Peel and remove the eyes from a fine ripe pineapple. Tear shreds from it with a fork and throw away the core. Sugar to taste, and serve ice cold, with floating island in separate dishes or on the same plates, as preferred.

In the opinion of many cooks, pineapples are more delicious and also more healthful if allowed to lie covered in wine, several hours before serving.

Bananas may be sliced and served with the floating island instead of pineapple; sugar to taste, pour orange juice over them, and serve ice cold.

The floating island must also be as cold as possible.

DUCK, ROASTED (THREE POUNDS).
ONION STUFFING.

Rinse the duck quickly in cold water, wipe, and stuff with a quart of bread-crumbs moistened with one cup of water, and the following seasoning: one half a teaspoonful of pepper, two teaspoonfuls of thyme, a half-teaspoonful of salt, one heaping teaspoonful of butter, one tablespoonful of chopped fat salt pork, and one small onion finely minced. Sew up with coarse thread, pepper, salt, and dredge with flour, and roast two hours (covered) in a moderate oven.

The duck should be placed on a meat-rack, and a cup of boiling water must be poured in the pan when it goes in the oven.

Stew the giblets in a cupful of boiling water, chop, add salt, a teaspoonful of flour, stir in the water they were cooked in, and add to the gravy in the roasting-pan.

POTATO BALLS (BAKED).

Take mashed potatoes seasoned for the table, form into egg-shaped rolls, and brown in a hot oven on a buttered tin.

These make an attractive border for a platter of meat.

BAKED CORN-STARCH LEMON MERINGUE PUDDING.

Heat one cupful of milk, and when at the boiling point stir in an even tablespoonful of corn-starch blended with a teaspoonful of best butter; cook one minute, stirring constantly, and add the yolk of one egg beaten with two tablespoonfuls of granulated sugar, the grated rind of a quarter and the juice of half a lemon, and a pinch of salt.

Pour this mixture into an earthen baking-dish and bake twenty minutes.

Take from the oven, add the white of the egg whisked to a stiff froth, to which has been added, after frothing, three tablespoonfuls of sugar and a tiny pinch of salt. Brown delicately in the oven and serve cold.

CHOCOLATE JELLY WITH CUSTARD.

Soak, then melt, four heaping teaspoonfuls of gelatine in two tablespoonfuls of cold water.

Add one cupful of boiling water, two pinches of salt, and two rounded tablespoonfuls of granulated sugar.

Melt in a double boiler one square of chocolate, then add two tablespoonfuls of boiling water, stir and cook until thick (time, about a quarter of a minute).

Now add very gradually, stirring constantly, half a cupful of boiling water, and when perfectly smooth, take from the fire; when cool, stir in the cooled gelatine, set in a pan of ice-water, and stir from the bottom and sides until thick enough to prevent the chocolate from settling.

Pour into a mould, set on ice, and when solid, serve with a custard made in the following way:

Beat the yolks of two eggs with two tablespoonfuls of granulated sugar and a pinch of salt; add one cupful of boiling milk and cook in the double boiler five minutes (longer cooking may curdle the mixture). Add half a teaspoonful of vanilla, or a spoonful of brandy or cordial, or any flavoring preferred. (Lemon, rose, or almond does not blend well with chocolate.)

Use the whites of the eggs in the following for another meal.

BAKED APPLES WITH MERINGUE.

Peel six Greening or Baldwin apples, core, fill with sugar, cover, and bake in a hot oven. When nearly done, remove the cover, brown and pile upon each apple a spoonful of frothed white of eggs beaten with one cup of sugar. Return to the oven and brown lightly.

Serve very cold.

XXVI.

Consommé with green peas.
Ham, baked, with or without tomatoes.
Hashed or stewed potatoes. Cream gravy.
Fried cabbage. Fried apples.
Hot biscuits with butter.
Olives.

String-bean salad.
Cream cheese. Biscuits.
Rice pudding, baked,
or
Baked apples, cream and sugar,
or
Sultana pudding.
Chocolate, tea, or coffee. Fruit.

CONSOMMÉ WITH GREEN PEAS.

Heat one and one half cupfuls of stock seasoned with onions, carrots, and the savory soup herbs. Add a tablespoonful of cooked peas, and two lengths of spaghetti broken into inch pieces.

Any other diced or small vegetable may be substituted for the peas.

BAKED SMOKED HAM.

One slice of ham one inch thick.

When found too salt ham may be made very palatable by soaking for an hour in a cupful of sweet milk. Cut off the rind and put the ham in an earthen pudding-dish which is just large enough to hold it without folding. Sprinkle over it an even teaspoonful of granulated sugar, a dust of pepper, and a teaspoonful of flour. Cover closely and bake in a slow oven two hours; then add the cupful of milk in which it was soaked, unless the milk has curdled, in which case substitute fresh, boil up once, and serve in the dish it was baked in or on a deep platter.

Ham baked with tomatoes, either fresh or canned, is a most appetizing dish, the acid of the tomato and the salt of the ham blending most agreeably.

After freshening, sugaring, and dredging with flour, place on top of the slice of ham a large tomato, skinned and sliced.

Dredge this also with flour and pepper, and bake. A spoonful of butter may be added if the ham is not very fat; the fatter the ham the sweeter and more tender it will be. Do not use the milk in which the ham was freshened, with tomatoes.

HASHED OR STEWED POTATOES. CREAM GRAVY.

Slice very thin a heaping cupful of cold baked potatoes; dredge with a teaspoonful of flour, a third of a teaspoonful of salt, and a dust of pepper.

Put a heaping teaspoonful of butter in a saucepan with a half-cupful of milk, and when hot, add the potatoes, stir once, and cook covered, about eight minutes, without further stirring; the slices should lie lightly in the gravy and be unbroken.

Water will not take the place of milk, which must be fresh and rich. If milk is not at hand, fry the potatoes in a little butter.

FRIED CABBAGE.

Cut into shavings enough cabbage to fill a quart measure; sprinkle with an even half-teaspoonful of salt, pour on two cups of boiling water, and cook rapidly until the cabbage becomes dry. Then add a tablespoonful of butter, two of milk, dust with pepper, and fry brown. Serve hot.

FRIED APPLES.

Slice two large Greening apples with a teaspoonful of melted butter. Pour over a dessertspoonful of water, and two heaping tablespoonfuls of sugar. Put dots of butter all over the top (a piece as large as a pea every two inches apart), cover closely, and fry gently without stirring until the bottom of the apples is a rich brown.

If cooked too fast they will burn and be bitter; twenty minutes or half an hour slow cooking will be about right. Cook in an earthen dish or agate pie plate.

BAKING-POWDER BISCUITS.

One cupful of flour sifted with one teaspoonful of baking-powder and one fourth of a teaspoonful of salt. Cut into this one heaping tablespoonful of butter and add a half-cupful of milk. Dredge with flour, cut into small pieces, pat each one into a ball, flatten lightly and lay them in a greased pan as close together as possible, and bake at once in a hot oven; fifteen minutes will be about the right time. This is the rule for pot-pies and stew-pies, although less shortening is required for these.

Pot-pies are made of meat, stew-pies of fruit. The dough is steamed on top of the meat (or fruit) instead of being baked as for biscuits. Time, about ten minutes. This dough is also called crust or dumplings. For pot-pie it is put in after the meat is done.

For stew-pies, put the fruit in a kettle with sugar and a dust of flour with a few spoonfuls of water, lay the crust, made into little walnut-shaped balls, on top ; cover the pot closely, and as soon as boiling begins, count the time.

Remember it is the steam which cooks dumplings ; if the dough is submerged in the juices or gravy it will be soggy.

In serving, use plenty of gravy, and make an extra sauce for the stew-pies.

One half of the rule is enough for two persons. Suet makes a delicious shortening, using a little more salt, and ice-water instead of milk.

STRING-BEAN SALAD.

Wash a dozen fresh, crisp string-beans, and steam in a steamer until tender.

Pull off the strings, salt, and serve them whole, on a lettuce leaf.

Garnish with a raw tomato sliced.

Use any dressing preferred.

RICE PUDDING (BAKED).

Stir into a pint of rich, fresh milk two heaping tablespoonfuls of granulated sugar, a saltspoonful of salt, and one tablespoonful of rice. Flavor with lemon rind, grated from a quarter of a lemon, and nutmeg.

Bake in an earthen dish in a very slow oven three hours. Keep the dish covered until the last twenty minutes.

Serve very cold.
Add more salt, if needed, before baking.

BAKED APPLES WITH CREAM.

Wipe carefully four Greening apples of equal size. Baldwins or Spitzenbergs will answer, but Greenings are best.

Remove the cores from the blossom end, making a little well in each ; use an apple-corer or a broad knife rounded at the end of the blade.

Place the apples in a deep earthen pie dish, and put a heaping tablespoonful of granulated sugar in each apple with an extra spoonful over all.

Pour on the bottom of the dish a half-cup of boiling water, set in a moderate oven, and bake from an hour to an hour and a half, according to the size of the apples and the heat of the oven.

When done, place them carefully in the dish they are to be served in, and when cold pour over them the jelly that exuded while baking. Do not make the mistake of not eating the skins. If the apples have been cooked slowly enough, the skins will be deliciously tender and rich.

Serve with cream and powdered sugar.

SULTANA PUDDING

One cupful of flour, one teaspoon baking-powder, one third of a teaspoon salt, one cupful Sultana raisins, one half-cupful rich milk, one tablespoonful sugar, yolk of one egg.

Sift flour, salt, and baking-powder together several times, and stir in the raisins, which have been picked over, rinsed, and dried in the oven.

Stir egg and milk together, add sugar, and then the flour, etc.

Steam for an hour in a buttered mould; cover the steamer, but leave the mould open. Serve with a sauce made of one cupful of confectioner's sugar, a scant half-cupful of butter, and brandy to taste. Add the frothed white of the egg, and beat about ten minutes.

CHOCOLATE.

Put one cupful of rich milk into a saucepan, add one third of a square of chocolate, and cook, stirring constantly (using a wooden or silver spoon), until the chocolate is all dissolved.

Use a double kettle, or a saucepan set in another of boiling water. Chocolate should never be grated, but put into *cold* milk in large pieces; grating results in loss of oil and flavor. One and one half squares will make a quart.

Do not use any water.

A spoonful of whipped cream added to each cup when serving is an elegant addition.

Sweeten to taste.

XXVII.

Corn soup.

Pot-roast (under-round or cross-rib).
Fried potatoes.   Stewed tomatoes.
Bread and butter.
Olives.   Grape or crab-apple jelly.
Lettuce or cauliflower.   Hollandaise sauce.
Cream cheese.   Brown-bread fingers.
Huckleberry or squash pie, or banana pudding meringue.
Tea or coffee.   Fruit.

Alternative: Broiled chicken or porter-house steak (broiled).
Charlotte russe or queen's pudding.

CORN SOUP.

Chop, or grate, a cupful of corn, add a slice of onion, a dessert-spoonful of butter, and an even teaspoonful of flour. Boil these in a pint of milk ten minutes, and then pour it upon an egg lightly beaten, stirring briskly. Add salt and pepper to taste, and strain back into the saucepan; boil up once, take from the fire immediately, or the egg will curdle, and serve with small oyster-crackers.

POT-ROAST.

(Under-round or cross-rib, two pounds.)

Trim the meat free of all dried skin and dried fat, and brown all sides in a hot spider; then put it in an agate-ware pot, pour on one cupful of boiling water, cover closely, and boil for a minute; turn the meat, and boil the other side. This is necessary, in order to seal up the rich juices of the meat, which would otherwise drip out into the gravy, leaving the meat dry and tasteless. Remove the meat to a platter, put in the pot a meat-rack tall enough to have its upper side at least two inches above the surface of the water, to prevent the meat from coming in contact with the water when it boils.

Dredge the meat all over with flour, dust on black pepper, place it on the rack, cover the pot closely, and cook gently, but steadily, three hours, adding more water occasionally from the boiling-kettle if it cooks away.

Always try to keep the original amount of water (one cupful).

Three or four pepper-corns may be added.

At the end of two and a half hours, add a half-teaspoonful of salt, sprinkling it over the meat, and a tablespoonful of parsley.

Remove the rack, and stir into the gravy a dessert-spoonful of flour blended with a few spoonfuls of cold water, and salt to taste. Recover the pot, and resume the cooking, only simmering gently for this last half-hour. Serve the meat on a warm platter, garnished with parsley or celery, and put the gravy in a sauce-boat. If fat is desired, fry delicately a piece of suet, and place beside the meat.

For a second meal, cook two lamb's kidneys (chopped) in a cupful of water, with one sliced onion, a tablespoonful of fried, diced, salt pork, a pinch of cayenne, salt to taste, and flour to thicken. Add the pot-roast, and boil up.

Pass cold spiced tomato sauce.

FRIED POTATOES.

Heat very hot a tablespoonful of drippings from salt pork, or the same amount of butter, being careful not to let them burn. Slice two medium-sized potatoes (baked or boiled) in quarter inch slices, and fry a rich brown, uncovered. If the pan is covered the potatoes will be flabby instead of crisp.

After dishing, sprinkle with salt and pepper and serve immediately. If preferred the potatoes may be broiled.

Spread each side of the slices with butter, and broil over a clear hot fire; season with salt and pepper and an extra lump of butter before serving.

CAULIFLOWER, HOLLANDAISE OR CREAM SAUCE.

Cut a fourth of a medium-sized cauliflower in four parts, salt, and steam, until tender, in a steamer, or wrap in a napkin and boil in a quart of boiling water (salted) twenty minutes.

Serve with Hollandaise sauce, or make a cream sauce of a tablespoonful of butter blended with a teaspoonful of flour and cooked with a half-cup of boiling milk.

Add a pinch of salt and a dust of pepper.

Pour the cream over the cauliflower and lay a slice of lemon on each piece.

Fine white cabbage may be boiled and served the same way.

Serve as a separate course with brown bread cut in finger-lengths.

SQUASH PIE.

Cut in half, scrape out the seeds, and peel one part of a Hubbard squash.

Steam until tender in a steamer, or boil in salted water.

Mash fine; a heaping cupful will make the pie. Put the rest away for other pies, or to use as a vegetable; it will keep several days in a cold place in cool weather.

Line a pie dish with pie-crust and bake as directed for other pies, while beating the yolk of an egg with four tablespoonfuls of granulated sugar, a half-teaspoonful of ground ginger, a half-teaspoonful of salt, and two thirds of a cup of hot milk poured on slowly, stirring all the time. Add a heaping teaspoonful of butter and a heaping cup of the hot mashed squash, a half-teaspoonful of flour, and a little grated nutmeg. Beat all together, and add the white of the egg beaten to a stiff froth. Beat thoroughly, pour into the pie pan, sprinkle with a teaspoonful of sugar, and bake in a quick oven ten or fifteen minutes.

HUCKLEBERRY PIE.

Use two large, deep saucers, as these will hold plenty of juice. Put in each one a cupful of huckleberries which have been looked over and washed.

Sprinkle with a tablespoonful of sugar, and the same of water, and cover with a flaky crust a little smaller than the top of the saucer ; bake twenty minutes in a hot oven.

Heat, mash, and strain through a coarse cloth wrung out of cold water, either a cupful of ripe currants or blackberries, and mix with this juice nearly a cupful of sugar, into which has been stirred a teaspoonful of flour. Cook a minute, and when the pies come from the oven, raise the crust and pour this juice over the huckleberries.

Replace the crust and serve either hot or cold.

BANANA PUDDING MERINGUE.

Beat the yolk of one egg with two tablespoonfuls of sugar and a quarter of a teaspoonful of salt; add the juice of half a tart orange and a cupful of milk, and pour this over a cupful of bread-crumbs (two or three days old) and one banana sliced and laid in alternate layers in a deep earthen pudding-dish. Bake twenty minutes in a hot oven.

Whisk the white of the egg to a stiff froth, add two tablespoonfuls of sugar, and after beating well, add the juice from the remainder of the orange and a pinch of grated rind; spread this upon the pudding and brown in the oven a few minutes.

BROILED CHICKEN.

Order a plump young chicken split for broiling. Wipe with a towel, and brush all over inside and out with melted butter or olive oil. Lay it on a broiler over a slow fire and broil twenty minutes, turning often to prevent burning.

Cook the inside first, to seal up the juices.

Lay, now, on a small rack (skin side down) in a spider which contains a large spoonful of butter and a half-cup of hot water; cover closely and simmer twenty minutes to a half-hour, or bake in the oven for the same length of time. Sprinkle with salt and pepper, add a little parsley, and pour over any juice or butter left in the spider.

If the chicken is not tender, simmer longer, with the addition of a little water, if it boils away. Any left over may be re-heated on the broiler.

PORTER-HOUSE STEAK (BROILED).

A medium-sized porter-house steak one and a quarter inches in thickness will make three meals for two moderate eaters, two broils and a hash.

Lay the steak on the meat-board, and with a sharp knife trim off the outer edge of the fat, which is always bitter from long contact with the air. Do not take off more than is necessary, as steak without a supply of fat is not delicious. Broil a piece of suet extra if it lacks a sufficient quantity.

Cut off the long coarse end, and remove the bone. Divide the remainder into two even portions, and put away one for another meal.

Broil the piece that is left, using a wire broiler in which the wires are about a third of an inch apart.

If a heavy iron broiler is used, it must be thoroughly heated before the meat goes on it. Have the fire a glowing, but not a fierce bed of coals. A fierce fire burns and hardens the meat before it is cooked through.

Do not use the broiler door with which most ranges are supplied, but remove the lid from the hottest place of the range and set the steak here to broil.

To keep the smoke from entering the house, open all the draughts, and put a tin cover over the broiler; every time the steak is turned with one hand, the cover is lifted with the other.

Broiled meats should be seared immediately to keep in the juices.

Count at first one hundred for each side; if the fire is very hot, fifty counts will be enough to begin on; then turn every ten counts, until four hundred have been counted. A steak an inch thick will most likely be done by this time, but to be certain open the broiler, and cut into the meat with a sharp knife; if not done enough, broil a few turns longer.

To be properly cooked it should be brown without, pink inside, and the gravy which runs from the cut should be red.

Have the platter warmed but not hot, sprinkle the steak with salt, and add butter the size of a walnut.

The steak is the last thing to be cooked for the meal, and everything else should be ready before beginning to broil it.

Serve immediately.

Here are several ways of treating the coarse end for little breakfast dishes.

Reduced to a pulp by passing it through a meat-grinder (or chopped in the chopping-bowl) it may then be made into a round flat cake and broiled the same as the steak, or fried and served with fried onions.

If broiled, serve with two slices of salt pork fried a delicate brown, and potatoes sliced and browned in the grease from the pork.

Put the meat in the centre of a platter and arrange the potatoes around it with slices of lemon as a garnish.

Another way is to fry it (the coarse end) in a small closely covered vessel until it is so tender that it can be cut without tearing. This will take from an hour to an hour and a half. Turn frequently and fry slowly. The edge of fat surrounding it will furnish enough grease for frying.

When cold, trim off the fat and throw it away; chop the meat fine, dredge with flour, add salt and pepper, and warm up with a few spoonfuls of milk or water, and a teaspoonful of butter.

Place upon toasted bread dipped in boiling, salted water, and then buttered. Pour over all hot spiced tomato sauce or sauce espagnole, and serve with fried potatoes. Ends of lamb chops may be cooked in the same way. Another way is to put the bone into water and boil until the scraps of meat and gristle drop away, then remove the bone, add a tablespoonful of browned salt pork without the grease, an inch of carrot, a slice of onion, and the coarse end of the steak.

Cook gently about two hours, keeping the meat barely covered with water. Then remove the vegetables, add salt to taste, and when cold take off the fat. Chop with one third as much cold potato, dredge with flour, and warm up with gravy in which the meat was cooked. This is a delicious hash.

SPICED TOMATO SAUCE TO BE SERVED WITH COLD MEATS, STEWS OR HASH.

1 onion chopped fine, 1 quart of ripe tomatoes, 1 small red-pepper pod or half of an even teaspoonful of cayenne, 1 teaspoonful of salt, 2 teaspoonfuls of sugar, 1 teaspoonful of mixed ground spices (mace, cloves, allspice, and cinnamon), 1 cupful of genuine cider vinegar.

Boil tomatoes and vinegar together two hours.

The tomatoes should be skinned and sliced if fresh ones are used.

Add onion and other ingredients and cook another hour.

If a smooth sauce is liked strain through a sieve. Keep in a cool place, covered.

CHARLOTTE RUSSE.

Place slices of stale cake in a covered dish, and set in a steamer until they become soft.

When cold, arrange on a dish for the table, and pour over them Sea-foam cream flavored with wine.

If preferred, whipped cream sweetened and flavored may be used instead. Sea-foam must stand on the ice awhile, but the whipped cream may be used immediately.

Substitute for whipped cream must also stand on ice to thicken.

QUEEN'S PUDDING.

Scald one cupful of milk, and soak in it one fourth of a cupful of bread-crumbs while beating the yolk of an egg, with two even tablespoonfuls of granulated sugar, a pinch of salt, and the grated rind of a quarter of a lemon.

Stir all together and bake in an earthen pudding-dish about fifteen minutes. Then spread on top a layer of jam, jelly, marmalade, or any rich preserves (using half a cupful), and on top of this the frothed white of the egg, sweetened, after frothing, with two tablespoonfuls of granulated sugar, and the juice of a quarter of a lemon. Return to the oven and brown (time, about seven minutes).

Serve cold, but not ice cold.

This becomes a new pudding with each change of preserves. The bread-crumbs are from the bread which is dried in the oven and then rolled to a powder on the moulding-board. Measure after rolling, and be exact in measuring.

XXVIII.

Raw oysters.

Roast turkey.

Mashed potatoes. Boiled onions.

Cranberry sauce.

Bread and butter. Celery.

Salted almonds or olives.

Lettuce if desired.

Cream cheese and wafers.

Orange jelly (ice cold).

Plum pudding.

Pineapple jardinière.

Coffee. Cream candies.

This menu is for Christmas Day.

That for Thanksgiving is the same, substituting mince pie for plum pudding.

ROAST TURKEY.

Select a fat turkey weighing nine or ten pounds. After it has been drawn, trimmed, and singed, rinse quickly in cold water and fill both cavities with stuffing, breaking the neck and turning it into the upper one.

Sew with a large darning-needle threaded with coarse darning-cotton, tie the legs together close to the body, and treat the wings the same way. Rub the outside of the turkey with salt, sprinkle over pepper and a tablespoonful of thyme, dredge plentifully with flour, lay on a meat-rack in a large dripping-pan, pour in two cups of water, and roast in a moderate oven from three to six hours, according to age. Lay a pan over the top to keep in the steam and juices; this must be removed the last hour if the turkey is not brown enough.

When half the time is up, turn the turkey over.

If thin slices of fat salt pork are laid on top there will be no need for basting.

The stuffing for a nine-pound turkey will require three quarts of bread-crumbs a few days old, and about a pint of boiling water (a little more if the bread is very dry), two heaping tablespoonfuls of thyme, a heaping teaspoonful of salt, a heaping teaspoonful of black pepper, a heaping tablespoonful of butter, and the same amount of the turkey-fat, chopped.

Mix all together thoroughly with the hand, see that all the lumps are dissolved and that butter, thyme, salt, and pepper are evenly distributed. The mixture should be quite soft, but not soft enough to run.

Put the gizzard in the dripping-pan when the turkey goes in; it can hardly be cooked too much if kept under water; turn it frequently and keep an inch of water in the pan, pouring in from the boiling teakettle as it cooks away.

Boil the heart and liver in a half-pint of water thirty minutes, and, when cold, chop in the chopping-bowl with the gizzard (very fine).

Blend two tablespoonfuls of flour with enough cold water to make it like cream, pour this in the dripping-pan after the turkey is removed, add the chopped giblets with the water they were cooked in and an extra cupful of boiling water, cook a few minutes, skim off most of the fat, and serve.

Put the turkey on a large platter garnished with celery.

Keep the turkey-fat, covered, in a cold place, and use it for frying potatoes.

CRANBERRY SAUCE (STRAINED).

Pick over and wash a pint of cranberries. Put them on a slow fire in an earthen vessel with a cup of cold water. Cover and cook gently two hours.

Then mash and strain through a coarse cloth. Add a cup of sugar, return to the fire, cook a few minutes, pour into a dish, and serve cold.

A quart of cranberries will be needed for a dozen people.

CRANBERRY SAUCE (WHOLE).

Pick over and wash two cupfuls of fine cranberries. Put them in an earthen dish, pour over a cup of sugar, add a cupful of boiling water, cover, and cook gently nearly two hours. Serve hot or cold.

ORANGE JELLY.

Soak four rounded teaspoonfuls of gelatine in two tablespoonfuls of water ten minutes.

Add three tablespoonfuls of sugar, a scant cupful of boiling water, and half a cupful of tart orange juice. Altogether this should measure one and a half cupfuls.

If only sweet oranges are obtainable, add a spoonful of lemon juice to give the required acidity. Add a few grains of salt and a pinch of grated orange rind. In hot weather use five teaspoonfuls of gelatine.

When this dish is used as a dessert, serve with it whipped cream, or Sea-foam cream.

GENUINE ENGLISH PLUM PUDDING.

One half-pound each of bread-crumbs,* kidney suet, brown sugar, Zante currants, table raisins, assorted candied fruits (lemon and orange peel and citron weighing half a pound altogether), sultana raisins (one pound), five eggs, one tablespoonful of flour, four tablespoonfuls molasses,

* Weigh the bread-crumbs before drying.

one teaspoonful of salt (rounded), one half-teaspoonful each of cinnamon and cloves, and a quarter of a nutmeg, one teaspoonful of ginger, one half-cupful of wine or brandy, or cider, if preferred. Wine or brandy makes a finer pudding, however.

Sift flour and spices together and chop in the suet. Add the candied fruit and chop as fine as peas.

Pick over carefully one by one the currants, wash in cold water, changing this until no sand is seen on the bottom of the dish, skimming the fruit out.

Then pour over them enough boiling water to barely cover and let them stand to swell.

Soak the table raisins in boiling water for a few minutes and take out the seeds. Pick over the sultanas and set them in the oven to get soft.

Now put all the fruit together and add the bread-crumbs, which must be stale, dried in the oven, and rolled to powder.

Beat up the eggs, add the sugar, molasses, and wine, and stir this well with the fruit, chopped suet, etc.

Butter three tin pails having covers, each holding a quart, and divide the pudding between them; it must have room to expand.

Steam steadily eight hours with water halfway up the sides.

Set the pails on wire tea-stands or a meat-rack.

Serve with brandy and hard sauces.

WINE SAUCE FOR PLUM PUDDING.

Cream half a cupful of best butter and one and a half cupfuls of light brown sugar until foamy, add two heaping tablespoonfuls of flour, beat and stir in slowly one and a half cups of boiling water and an even teaspoonful of salt.

Boil, stirring constantly, ten minutes, then add half a cupful of wine or brandy and serve hot in a sauce-boat. Color with a teaspoonful of caramel.

HARD SAUCE.

Cream half a cupful of butter, add one cupful of confectioner's sugar, beat fifteen minutes, and pile into a serving bowl.

Grate nutmeg over the top.

This quantity of sauce will be sufficient for twelve people.

Plum pudding improves with age. It must be kept closely covered in the pails in which it was cooked.

When wanted, cut off slices and heat (covered) in the oven, or in a steamer. Half a slice, half an inch thick, is enough for one portion.

Get the fruit and bread-crumbs ready for mixing the day before and cook the pudding at least a week before it is to be served. One of the puddings may be cut in half and frosted with a deep soft frosting and passed as fruit cake. It must be eaten with a fork, however, as it is too soft and sticky to be held in the fingers.

MINCE-MEAT FOR ONE LARGE PIE.

One gill of mixed candied citron, lemon, and orange peels, one gill of chopped suet, three gills of mixed raisins and currants, three gills chopped apples, raw, one cupful of chopped cooked beef, two tablespoonfuls molasses, three tablespoonfuls brown sugar, one heaping teaspoonful of mixed spices (nutmeg, allspice, cloves, cinnamon, and black pepper), one quarter of a teaspoonful salt, one cupful of cider or wine and cider mixed.

Cover the raisins with cold water and seed them. Pick over the currants and wash them, and cover both raisins and currants with cold water and cook slowly until the water has boiled off. Then add the candied fruit and suet (chopped fine), sugar, molasses, spices, and cider, and boil an hour, stirring frequently.

Mix apples and meat together, add salt and the other ingredients, and cook up thoroughly (about ten minutes). Put away in a jar until wanted.

The meat should be boiled or stewed until very tender, and well salted before it gets cold. Cover with boiling water and cook until the water is all gone, being careful not to scorch.

Under-round pot-roast will make good mincemeat, also stewing beef. Chop when cold.

A little brandy may be poured over the pie just before serving.

Raise the crust and allow a spoonful for each portion.

PINEAPPLE JARDINIÈRE.

Cut the top from a ripe pineapple and reserve it for the cover.

Cut out the inside, rejecting the core, and scoop out the juice and the part lying next to the rind, with a spoon, being careful not to break nor puncture it. Put the rind and the cover in a cool place. Put the pineapple into a bowl, add half a cupful of sherry (a few spoonfuls of brandy, rum, or champagne may be substituted for the sherry), and let it stand on ice until wanted at table, then mix with orange pulp, seeded and halved Tokay grapes, banana, or peaches and plums, stoned cherries, or berries according to season, sugar to taste, fill the rind, put on the cover, and set the pineapple on a dish of cracked ice. Serve in flaring champagne glasses.

One pineapple, two oranges, one banana, and half a pound of grapes will fill the rind twice and serve twelve people.

MENUS FOR COMPANY LUNCHEONS.

I.

Oyster cocktails.

Breaded French chops.   White sauce.
Mashed potatoes.   Celery.

Tomato mayonnaise.
Cheese.   Crackers.

Vanilla ice-cream.
Coffee.   Fruit.

II.

Grape fruit.

Beauregarde eggs.

Fried chicken.
Escalloped potatoes.
Stuffed tomatoes.

Lettuce salad.
Cream cheese.   Crackers.

Coffee Bavarian cream.
Fruit.   Coffee.

III.

Bouillon in cups.
French chops.   Green peas.
Fried potatoes.
Croustade of oysters.
Lettuce salad.
Crackers.   Cheese.
Vanilla ice-cream.   Caramel sauce.
Fruit.   Coffee.

IV.

Oysters on half-shell.
Fried smelts.   Sauce tartare.
Blanquette of chicken.
Mashed potatoes.
Tomato and celery salad.
Cheese.   Crackers.
Pineapple jardinière.
Coffee.

SUPPLEMENTARY DISHES IN COMPANY LUNCHEONS.

OYSTER COCKTAILS.

Oyster cocktails are served in small cocktail glasses, with a dressing of catsup, etc.

Order very small oysters, drain, and see that they are very cold and free from bits of shell.

Put half a dozen in each glass, and pour over them several spoonfuls of the dressing made as follows :

One tablespoonful of lemon juice, one tablespoonful of tomato catsup, half a teaspoonful of Worcestershire sauce, five drops of Tobasco sauce, and a little salt.

This quantity will be sufficient for three people, but the rule may be doubled or trebled according to need.

BREADED CHOPS.

The chops should be breaded and delicately fried, and arranged on a hot platter.

At the moment of serving, pour over a rich white sauce.

VANILLA ICE-CREAM.

Put one pint of milk in the double boiler with a piece of vanilla bean about an inch in length.

Cream together two eggs, half a cup of sugar, and two rounded tablespoonfuls of flour until very light, and stir gradually into the milk when it reaches the boiling point.

Allow this to cook ten minutes, stirring frequently. Add a small pinch of salt, and turn into a stone dish, beating at intervals while it cools to prevent it from forming into lumps.

When cold add one and a half pints of cream (or rich *country* milk) and half a cup of sugar.

This mixture may be prepared early in the day and kept in the ice-box.

If a larger quantity is desired, a quart of cream may be used, the foundation being the same.

Care must be taken in measuring the flour, as too much is sure to taste ; the spoon must be *rounding* full instead of heaping—about one ounce in all.

Be sure and use the vanilla bean for flavoring, as it is quite impossible to make a good ice-cream with vanilla extract.

All large grocery houses keep vanilla in this form, and it would doubtless be easy to have one or more sent by post to any place where they were not obtainable.

Before freezing, remove the bit of pod, carefully scraping all the little seeds into the custard.

Prepare the ice by pounding it fine in a coarse, strong bag, and use rock salt in the proportion of three pints for a gallon freezer.

Put the can in the centre of the tub with the beater in place, fasten the lid securely, and pack ice and salt in alternate layers until the tub is full.

Turn the crank a few minutes, and as the ice works down, add more, until it is firmly and solidly packed.

If plenty of ice is used, twenty minutes will serve to freeze the cream.

The crank need not be turned constantly, and the motion at first should be rather slow. When the custard begins to harden, turn rapidly, as this is the stage when rapid beating makes the cream smooth and light.

When it is firm enough, take out the paddle, beat well with a wooden spoon to fill up the space made by the beater, and scrape well from the sides.

Cover the tub with a blanket and set away in a cool place, and let two hours elapse before serving.

When ready to do so, dip the can in warm (not hot) water, wipe dry, and invert on a cold dish.

It should come out in firm and perfect shape.

It is possible to have several varieties of cream in the same mould with only one freezing, and various combinations may be made to suit the individual taste.

After the cream is frozen a portion may be taken out into a cold bowl and a cupful of well-sweetened strawberry or raspberry juice stirred into it. Pour this back into the can and it will soon harden to the proper consistency.

A quarter of a cupful of very strong coffee may be used in the same way.

A banana or two may be sliced thin and added as another variation, or a little shredded pineapple.

Ripe peaches, if cut up and sweetened, may also be used, but they should not be added until about half an hour before serving-time, as they should only be chilled and not frozen.

Candied fruits, particularly apricots and cherries, are also a pleasant addition, if cut into very minute pieces and well mixed through the cream.

GRAPE FRUIT.

Grape fruit should be well chilled, cut in half, the core removed, and the pulp loosened slightly around the outside edge; use a sharp knife and be careful not to let any of the white part adhere, as this is very bitter.

Fill the core cavity with cracked ice and sugar and serve a half to each person, on a pretty plate.

These may be on the table when the meal is announced.

This course is eaten with orange-spoons or the ordinary teaspoon.

BEAUREGARDE EGGS.

Boil six eggs twenty minutes. Make a pint of cream sauce. Cut the whites of the eggs in thin strips, mix with the sauce, and fill baking shells, one for each person.

Rub the yolks of the eggs through a sieve on top of each shell, put in the oven for two or three minutes, and serve.

OYSTER CROUSTADE.*

Get a round loaf of baker's bread which is two or three days old, and scoop out all the crumb, being careful not to break the crust.

Break up the crumbs very fine and dry them slowly in the oven.

When dry, fry three cupfuls in two tablespoonfuls of butter, stirring all the time (about three minutes).

Put one quart of cream, or rich milk, on the fire, and when it reaches the boiling point stir in three tablespoonfuls of flour which have been mixed with half a cupful of cold milk. Cook for a few minutes and season with salt and pepper.

Now put a layer of this sauce in the loaf, then a layer of oysters salted and peppered, another layer of sauce, and then one of the fried crumbs.

Repeat this until the croustade is nearly full, having a thick layer of crumbs on top.

Bake slowly half an hour and serve with a garnish of parsley.

Three pints of oysters are required for this dish, but half the quantity of ingredients given will be sufficient when the croustade is to form a single course.

CARAMEL CREAM SAUCE.

Caramel sauce is made by stirring into a cup-

* Miss Parloa.

ful of cold cream two tablespoonfuls of caramel, directions for which have been given elsewhere.

Serve in a pretty bowl and pass to each guest.

A pint or more of caramel may be made at a time and bottled; it will keep indefinitely.

OYSTERS ON THE HALF-SHELL.

Four or five small oysters on the half-shell are sufficient for each portion.

Arrange on a small plate on a bed of cracked ice with a quarter of a lemon in the centre.

Pass horse radish and crackers with this course.

FRIED SMELTS.

The smelts should be breaded some time before the meal, and fried either in deep fat or in a little beef dripping, until a delicate brown.

Serve with a sauce tartare, which is a mayonnaise with an addition of chopped pickles and capers.

BLANQUETTE OF CHICKEN.*

One quart of cooked chicken, cut in delicate pieces; one large cupful of white stock, three tablespoonfuls of butter, a heaping tablespoonful of flour, one teaspoonful of lemon juice, one cupful of cream or milk, the yolks of four eggs, salt, pepper.

* Miss Parloa.

Put the butter into the saucepan, and when hot, add the flour.

Stir until smooth, but do not let it brown. Add the stock and cook two minutes, then add the seasoning and cream.

As soon as this boils up add the chicken and cook ten minutes.

Beat the yolks of the eggs with four tablespoonfuls of milk ; stir into the blanquette and cook about half a minute longer.

This may be served in a rice border or with a garnish of toasted bread.

TOMATO AND CELERY SALAD.*

Select firm, good-sized ripe tomatoes. Cut a lid from the top and scoop out all the seeds and soft pulp with a spoon, being very careful not to break the tomato. Mix celery cut as for salad in small pieces, with mayonnaise dressing.

Fill the tomatoes with this mixture, put a teaspoonful of dressing on the top of each tomato, and serve on crisp lettuce leaves.

Table Talk.

BREAKFAST, TEA, AND LUNCHEON DISHES.

EGGS AU GRATIN FOR LUNCHEON.

Heat one third of a cupful of milk with a tablespoonful of butter in a broad, shallow baking-dish. Put into this four muffin-rings and break an egg into each ring; sprinkle with salt and pepper and add a layer of grated cheese. Brown delicately in a quick oven, or cook on top of the stove and brown the top with a hot stove-lid or red-hot shovel.

Eggs require only a few minutes' cooking.

A tiny pinch of mustard and cayenne may be added to the milk if liked.

SMOKED TONGUE.

Wash, cover with cold water, and soak overnight a fine beef tongue. Next morning put it into a two-gallon pot, cover with boiling water, and cook gently five or six hours.

When cold pull off the skin and slice in thin slices.

Any scraps that remain may be chopped,

mashed to a paste, seasoned with cayenne pepper, and used for sandwiches.

CRUST FOR OYSTER PATTIES.

Beat one fresh ice-cold egg with four tablespoonfuls of ice-water until it appears to be a mass of froth. Set it on the ice while cutting one cupful of ice-cold butter into two cupfuls of flour which have been sifted several times with a salt-spoonful of salt.

When the butter has been cut to the size of peas beat up again, quickly, the egg mixture, and with a spoon mix it into the flour. Beat with the rolling-pin and roll out an eighth of an inch thick, cut into circles the right size to fit in patty pans, cut covers, and bake in a quick oven.

The covers are baked on tins or dripping-pans.

Do not handle the paste more than is absolutely necessary; simply pinch it together with the tips of the fingers, roll out once, and put in the oven as quickly as possible.

Make the paste in a cool room, and only roll out a portion at a time, keeping the rest in the ice-box.

Keep the trimmings separate, pinch them all together at the last, and roll out once. Take the last little scraps, form into balls, and roll each one out by itself for tarts.

This prevents too much working with the dough and also does away with the necessity of using too much flour.

If the butter softens before baking, the crust will not be crisp and flaky.

These patties will keep two weeks in a cool, dry place, and may be filled at any time and heated in the oven.

If oyster filling is desired, make a cream sauce of a tablespoonful of butter, an even teaspoonful of flour, the juice of a dozen small oysters, salt and pepper to taste, cook a few minutes, then add the oysters and a tablespoonful of cream, boil up once, and serve in the hot shells.

A little lemon and onion juice may be added.

For chicken patties, make the sauce of butter, flour, and milk, with the yolk of a hard-boiled egg mashed fine; add parsley and onion juice, salt and pepper, and minced chicken. The tart shells may be filled with jellies, marmalades, or preserved or rich stewed fruits.

SOUFFLÉS.
(Chicken or Fish.)

Take half a cupful of the white part of boiled chicken, pound to a paste, moisten with two tablespoonfuls of cream (or milk and butter), add the beaten yolk of a raw egg, season with parsley, mushrooms, or any preferred herb, salt and pepper to taste, add the frothed white of the egg, put quickly and lightly into a buttered mould, and either set in a hot oven for a few minutes, or in a saucepan of boiling water. Cook only long enough to set the egg; too much cooking will toughen and spoil a soufflé, which must be served and eaten the moment it comes from the fire. Put on a heated dish, and pour around it a sauce made from chicken broth, thickened with a little browned flour mixed with butter, and flavored either with mushrooms, onion, lemon juice, or wine.

Boiled fish may be used in the same way with a seasoning of anchovies, wine, and cayenne. Canned salmon is a very good basis for a soufflé, and the sauce of thin drawn butter may be improved by the addition of capers.

SALMON, WITH HOLLANDAISE SAUCE.

Canned salmon may be used for this dish, which will be found valuable in an emergency.

Heat a little butter in a frying-pan, and lay the salmon in it long enough to cook and heat thoroughly; then put it on a dish, salt and pepper to taste, and serve either with Hollandaise sauce, or cream sauce, or drawn butter, with parsley or capers.

BAKED HAMBURG STEAK.

A "meat-cutter" is a most valuable kitchen

utensil, and meat-balls and Hamburg steaks may be prepared very quickly with it. Remove all of the fat, tendons, and gristle from half a pound of round steak, pass this through the cutter, and then grind through a lump of fine kidney suet the size of a hen's egg.

Mix all together, smooth into a square mound, pepper, and dredge with flour, and bake in a quick oven, rare or well done, as preferred.

Serve with butter and salt, pouring off the grease first. This dish is delicious cold. Onion juice may be added if liked, also sliced lemon or watercress.

FRIZZLED BEEF.

Make a sauce of a dessert-spoonful of butter stirred to a cream with one of flour, add a cupful of boiling milk (water will do), stir, and cook several minutes; then add half a cupful of dried beef, torn into inch pieces, and set on the back of the range fifteen minutes to swell and get hot, but not cook.

Stir occasionally, and add a little more milk if it seems too thick or too salt. Pepper lightly, and serve with bread toasted, dipped in salted boiling water, and buttered liberally.

The toast should be on a separate dish.

Hot hard-boiled eggs make an excellent garnish.

REMNANTS OF COLD OVEN-ROASTS OR BROILS.

Take any oven-roast, steak or chops, and fry slowly two hours, or until tender, with a slice of fat salt pork ; or stew in just enough water to cover.

Be careful not to burn, and keep closely covered. When done, throw away the grease, trim off fat, gristle, and bones, cut the meat into mouthfuls, sprinkle with salt, pepper, butter, and flour, add a little water and beef extract, or any gravy at hand. Lay on top of the meat hot mashed potatoes, and brown in the oven.

For a change add a well-beaten egg to the potatoes (two cupfuls), and a little more milk.

Bake in a quick oven.

Boiled meats or pot-roasts will not need to be cooked before baking ; they are tender enough.

REMNANTS OF COLD POULTRY, VEAL, OR LAMB.

Mince the meat into pieces as large as large-sized peas; pick out all bone, gristle, fat, and skin, and mix with the following sauce : Mash the yolk of a hard-boiled egg with a tablespoonful of butter, a little salt, and a pinch of cayenne, and when it becomes a paste add a teaspoonful of flour. Pour on two thirds of a cupful of boiling milk, cook a few minutes, add the white of the egg, chopped fine, and then stir in the meat. Set on the stove long enough to heat, but not cook, and serve on thin slices of dipped and buttered toast.

Another way is to make a dressing of equal parts of cracker- or bread-crumbs and oysters, salt, pepper, and butter to taste; lay this on meat, and brown in oven.

Another way is to chop the meat fine, bind together with a thick drawn butter, form into flat cakes, dip into powdered cracker-crumbs (or beaten egg and cracker), and fry in a little butter or hot lard (salt to taste).

Still another way is to cut the meat in slices half an inch thick, trim off the fat, brush with milk or water (or dip into beaten egg), bread with powdered cracker-crumbs, and fry just long enough to brown outside.

Serve on a bed of watercress, and cover each cutlet with a thick sauce made of a little flour, cracker-crumbs, butter, boiling water, and lemon juice, or minced parsley.

Pass currant or grape jelly.

Roast pork may be made into cutlets, in which case pass crab-apple jelly or stewed apples. Saltine crackers are nice for breading.

ESPAGNOLE, OR BROWN SAUCE, FOR STEWS, ETC.

Fry one slice of onion (and a slice each of

carrot and turnip, adding parsley and celery if liked) in a tablespoonful of chopped salt pork or butter, until a rich brown.

Then add an even tablespoonful of flour, cook up, and add salt and a half-cupful of boiling water in which has been dissolved a quarter of a spoonful of beef extract.

Cook a few minutes and strain. Rich stock may be used instead of the extract.

This sauce may be made with the onion alone if the other vegetables are not at hand, and a half-teaspoonful of curry-powder converts it into a curry sauce.

ONION BUTTER.

For flavoring gravies, stews, and dishes of cooked-over meats, an onion butter is a great convenience, as it will keep for weeks in a cold place. This butter can be used where onion is objected to, even the most suspicious not being able to detect its presence.

Slice a large white onion and fry it in two tablespoonfuls of butter until the onion has shrivelled and turned brown.

Then strain through a wire strainer into a little earthen jar with a close cover. Throw away the onion. A quarter-teaspoonful of this is enough flavoring for a dish for two or three persons.

SWEETBREAD SALAD.

One pair of lamb sweetbreads will make enough salad for two people when served for dinner as a separate course, but more will be required for lighter meals. Pour boiling water on them, let stand for a few minutes, and then plunge them in ice-water.

When thoroughly chilled, pour on hot water to cover, bring to a boil, and cook gently about eight minutes.

They should be tender by this time.

Cool quickly by plunging again in ice-water, break into small pieces, removing all gristle and fat, and mix with cream salad dressing or mayonnaise. Serve on crisp lettuce leaves.

Veal sweetbreads will take about twenty minutes to cook, as they are much larger.

POTATO SALAD FOR TEA OR LUNCHEON.

Chop fine one cupful of cold baked potato and add the following sauce : Mix together one teaspoonful of butter, one even teaspoonful of flour, a pinch of mustard and one of cayenne, one third of a teaspoonful of salt, and then add half a cupful of boiling milk and a few drops of onion juice. Cook until creamy, then add the chopped potato and stir until the mass is heated through.

When cold, serve with hard-boiled eggs and French dressing.

This may be served with lettuce leaves or with a simple garnish of capers and parsley. Chopped meat is sometimes added to this salad, in the proportion of one third potatoes to two thirds meat.

SMOTHERED CHICKEN.

The chicken for this dish must be young, tender, and plump.

Have it split as for broiling.

Wipe dry with a cloth, spread it liberally with butter all over, dust with flour and pepper, and lay it, skin side down, on a meat-rack in a dripping-pan. Pour in a cupful of boiling water, add a few sprigs of parsley, cover closely, and bake in a hot oven thirty minutes, or longer if necessary.

Then turn the chicken skin side up, and brown uncovered ten or fifteen minutes.

Cut up the giblets, cooked tender in one cupful of water, add a spoonful of flour and a lump of butter the size of a hen's egg, add the water from the giblets, stir all in the dripping-pan, and cook, seasoning with salt, pepper, parsley, or sweet marjoram. Joint the chicken so it may be easily carved, but do not separate it. Serve on a platter with the gravy poured around.

PICKED-UP CODFISH.

Pour boiling water on half a pound of salt codfish picked into bits and bones removed. Pour the water off in a few minutes and cover with more. This will make the fish fresh enough when it is drained the second time.

Blend a tablespoonful of butter and a dessertspoonful of flour together, add half a cup of milk, and cook a few minutes. Then add the codfish and a little minced parsley, simmer a few minutes, and serve on a platter with a hard-boiled egg cut in slices distributed over the surface.

Add black pepper and capers if desired.

MAPLE-SUGAR SYRUP.

Break up one pound of genuine maple sugar, pour over it three cupfuls of boiling water, and set on back of the range to melt. Then strain through several thicknesses of cheese-cloth wrung out of water. Return to the fire and boil and skim half an hour. There should be one pint of syrup.

MILK TOAST.

Take dry pieces of bread, heat them in the oven, then toast a fine even brown. Dip into boiling salted water, butter, and place in a dish.

Boil a pint of rich milk and stir in it half a

teaspoonful of corn-starch (or flour) mixed with a heaping teaspoonful of butter; add salt to taste, and after cooking a few minutes pour over the toast.

CHEESE ON TOAST.

One half-cupful of old English cheese, grated; four tablespoonfuls of milk, one teaspoonful of butter, one even teaspoonful of flour, one pinch of salt. Blend flour and butter, add the milk, boil up, add the cheese, boil up again, and pour on toasted bread which has been dipped in salted boiling water and slightly buttered.

Set in the oven, covered, until wanted, but it should be served soon after it is ready.

FRESH FISH (FRIED).

(Any preferred kind. One pound.)

After cleaning and scaling, wash in cold water. Do this quickly and dry gently with a napkin. Either dredge with flour or dip in rolled cracker-crumbs (half a cup of crumbs will be required). Sprinkle on half a teaspoonful of salt and a dust of pepper, and fry a fine brown in any fat preferred. A tablespoonful of butter, or the grease from two slices of fat salt pork, will be sufficient.

Fry rapidly at first, then cook about ten minutes for each side on a cooler part of the stove.

Serve on a platter with lumps of butter dotting the fish. Roes of shad or mackerel are cooked the same way.

CODFISH BALLS.

Cut into inch pieces one heaping cupful of salt codfish. Remove the bones and skin and put into an earthen dish, pour on three cupfuls of boiling water, and set on the stove to keep warm, but not boil, for two hours. It should be freshened enough by this time. Pour off the water, pick into tiny bits, or chop, add one heaping cupful of hot mashed potato and the following drawn butter: Mix one teaspoonful of flour with one heaping tablespoonful of butter, add three tablespoonfuls of boiling water and a dust of pepper, and cook a few minutes.

Make into eight little flat cakes, dredge with flour, and fry (next day) a delicate brown, in salt-pork drippings. Serve on a platter with the slices of fried salt pork, garnished with parsley.

A border of hard-boiled eggs (hot) may be added.

SAUSAGES (FRIED AND BAKED).

Sausages should be well cooked; in fact pork in any form should never be served unless it is thoroughly well done.

Put the sausages in a pan, cover, and fry

slowly, turning from side to side until every part has come in contact with the fire. Add a little boiling water to the gravy, stir, boil up, and pour over the sausages.

If baked, more time will be required.

Have the oven quite hot. Some cooks prefer to cut each sausage in half, lengthwise, adding a little extra seasoning of sage and pepper.

OATMEAL.

One scant cupful of "pin-head" oatmeal, three and a half cupfuls of boiling water, and one even teaspoonful of salt.

Stir until it begins to boil, and in a little while stir again; then cover and cook slowly two hours.

In cool weather this will keep several days, and may be warmed up as required.

The "Universal" pot is the best utensil in which to cook oatmeal and hominy; it is a crock set in a bottomless tin frame.

Pin-head oatmeal is far superior to any of the steam-cooked oats.

INDIAN-MEAL MUSH.

Pour one pint of boiling water on one cupful of yellow Indian meal and a scant teaspoonful of salt.

Stir constantly to prevent lumping.

When well mixed, tie closely in a wet cloth and boil steadily two or three hours, or longer, in a pot of salted boiling water. Set a tea-stand in the bottom of the pot to prevent the cloth from sticking.

Turn into a dish, and when cold, slice, dredge with flour (or bread-crumbs), and fry in hot salt-pork drippings or butter.

Serve hot with butter and syrup.

MUFFINS.

(Baking-Powder.)

Sift one heaping cupful of flour with one teaspoonful of baking-powder and a scant half-teaspoonful of salt.

Beat one egg, and one cup of milk and water (half and half), one teaspoonful of sugar, a heaping tablespoonful of butter, melted; stir well, and then add the flour.

Bake in gem pans or muffin-rings twenty minutes in a hot oven.

POACHED EGGS.

Half fill a frying-pan with boiling water, put in a little salt and half a dozen muffin-rings.

Break the eggs, one at a time, in a saucer, and slip one into each muffin-ring.

Boil until the whites assume a milky color.

Serve on buttered toast which has been freed from crust.

A perforated skimmer should be used to take up the eggs.

They will require about one minute to cook.

SCRAMBLED EGGS.

Allow a teaspoonful of butter for each egg.

Heat the butter, add the eggs unbeaten, and stir, cooking slowly a few minutes ; they should be soft when taken from the fire, and a trifle juicy. If hard, the dish will be spoiled.

Serve immediately.

HAM OMELETTE.

Beat three eggs until whites and yolks are blended,—no longer ; eggs for omelettes do not require much beating.

Add a quarter of a cup of milk in which one heaping tablespoonful of finely powdered bread crumbs have soaked thoroughly, and a tablespoonful of melted butter.

Fry in a sheet-iron frying-pan, heated very hot, two minutes, drawing the omelette away from the sides of the pan so that the uncooked part can reach the fire.

Sprinkle with pepper, and lay over the top two tablespoonfuls of finely minced ham (either fried or boiled). Cover the pan until the ham is hot; then loosen the omelette with a broad knife-blade, and roll it up.

Serve at once.

Sliced raw tomatoes make an appetizing garnish for this dish. To be right the omelette must be soft inside ; too hot a fire, or too long cooking, will make it tough and hard. Bacon, freed from rind and fried delicately brown, chopped fine, may be used instead of ham. No butter will be required, as the omelette should be fried in the bacon-drippings.

If preferred, omelettes may be baked in a hot oven ; they should be left in just long enough to set the eggs.

BACON AND EGGS.

Fry the bacon a delicate brown.

Put the eggs into muffin-rings in the hot bacon fat (first removing the bacon), and baste them constantly with the fat until the white of the eggs becomes milk-white ; then serve, arranged around the bacon.

If liked, a gravy may be made of flour, bacon fat, and milk, and poured over.

Thirty seconds should cook the eggs.

LIVER AND BACON.

Fry a quarter of a pound of bacon, and when nicely browned, but not crisp, put it on a platter. Into the hot drippings put two slices of liver, floured and peppered. Cook about ten minutes, basting continually with the bacon fat.

Add one teaspoonful of flour to three tablespoonfuls of fat, and half a cup of boiling milk, to make a gravy; cook, and pour over the liver. A teaspoonful of lemon may be added, and a few drops of onion-juice if liked; in that case make the gravy of water.

Serve with dipped toast or pan-cakes.

Lamb's kidneys may be substituted for the liver; split them through the centre, remove the veins of fat, cover with cold water, boil until scum rises; skim; then drain and dredge with flour, and proceed the same as for liver; the water may be used for the gravy.

Lamb's kidneys may be fried in butter, and breaded, instead of floured, if preferred. They may also be served without the bacon.

BROILED FISH.

Flour the fish (which has been cleaned, rinsed, and dried) lightly, and broil on a well-greased gridiron over a clear but quiet fire, turning frequently enough to prevent burning.

It should take about half an hour to broil a fish one inch thick. Fish must be cooked slowly and thoroughly. Serve with butter, salt, and pepper to taste. Salt fish must be freshened by soaking over night in enough water to fully cover. Wipe dry before cooking.

Lemons, pickles, or parsley may be used as a garnish.

HAM ON TOAST.

Make a drawn-butter sauce; add some cold ham, finely minced, and as soon as it is warmed through spread on squares of dipped toast.

The dish may be garnished with poached eggs or sliced hard-boiled eggs.

After hard-boiled eggs are shelled they may be kept hot by putting them in a bowl of hot water until ready to serve.

One tablespoonful of minced ham is a portion. If fried ham is used, and any milk gravy remains, use that in the sauce. Use only enough sauce to make the ham stick together in a compact mass.

VEAL LOAF.

Fry one eighth of a pound of sliced salt pork. When delicately browned, but before it becomes crisp, put it, without the grease, into an agate, or the "Universal" pot, and arrange on top a pound of veal cut from the thick part of the leg.

Sprinkle some parsley on top, add a gill of water, cover closely, and simmer three hours. Set away to get cold, when chop into pieces the size of peas; remove the parsley. Add a pinch each of thyme, cayenne pepper, and black pepper, one teaspoonful of onion-juice, one well-beaten egg, a tablespoonful of melted butter, and the melted jelly from the meat.

Salt to taste, and pack smoothly in a baking-dish; if there is not enough jelly to make it moist and rather juicy, add a little water. Cover the top with bread crumbs, and bake slowly one hour, covered.

Slice cold, garnish with celery, and pass pickled peaches; or garnish with skinned ripe tomatoes or sliced lemon, and pass celery.

WHEAT AND INDIAN GRIDDLE-CAKES.

One overflowing cup of sour (loppered) milk, one scant half-level teaspoonful of soda, one well-beaten egg, one tablespoonful of butter (melted), two thirds of a teaspoonful of salt, three even tablespoonfuls of yellow corn meal, one half cup of flour measured before sifting. Mix half an hour before baking, and then add the soda dissolved in one teaspoonful of cold water.

Beat it in thoroughly and bake on a hot griddle.

In cold weather sour milk may be secured by setting fresh milk in a temperature of about 75° for a few days. Whip a few minutes before using to make it light and foamy.

Bread cakes are made in the same way by substituting bread crumbs for the flour, and flour for the meal. A pinch of salt will be sufficient for these.

If too thin add an extra spoonful of flour.

Prepare the bread crumbs in the following way:

Cut the crusts from stale bread, put both (crusts and inside) in the oven to dry; then roll to powder. The crusts, being brown, should be kept by themselves for browning the tops of dishes: the inside part is for griddle-cakes and puddings.

These cakes are delicious served for dessert at luncheon, with sugar and butter, or butter and maple-syrup.

QUICK BEEF-TEA.

Pass through the meat grinder, or chop very fine, one pound of round or stewing beef (raw) freed from fat before grinding. Put into a bowl, cover with one cupful of cold water, set in a saucepan of cold water and cook (after boiling begins) ten minutes, stirring occasionally. Strain through a *coarse* sieve, and add salt and pepper to taste. If too strong add a *little* more water to the meat and cook up again. Beef-tea is apt to be too weak as it is generally made; therefore be careful not to add too much water; a few spoonfuls is enough.

TO BOIL NEW POTATOES.

New potatoes are at their best when baked, but they can generally be made light and mealy if the following rules are observed. Scrape off the skin, cut in three-quarter-inch slices, soak in cold water a few minutes and then put them into rapidly boiling (salted) water, cover until hard boiling begins, then partly uncover. They must boil continuously and vigorously. When done, drain, spread a muslin over the potatoes, replace the cover and shake the pot up and down several times as violently as possible : the potatoes will be broken and they will lie in a drifting, snowy mass.

Set on the stove a minute only, covered with the muslin; then put into a heated dish, sprinkle with salt and pepper and keep hot covered with muslin until ready to serve.

BAKED HASH.

Hash may be baked in the oven until it is a fine brown on top. Cooked in this way it makes a nice dinner dish if garnished.

Serve in baking-dish, or slip it onto a platter, and border with potatoes sliced, breaded with bread crumbs, and fried a rich brown in a spoonful of salt-pork drippings.

GRAHAM MUFFINS.

Follow the rule for Raised Steamed Dumpling, substituting two cupfuls of Graham flour for the one cupful of white flour and use molasses instead of sugar.

Raise and bake in patty-pans instead of steaming.

SARDINE SALAD.

Lay the sardines upon brown paper to absorb the oil. Scrape off the skin and remove the bones, and squeeze lemon juice over them.

Arrange them upon crisp lettuce leaves and serve with either French or mayonnaise dressing.

Sliced hard-boiled eggs make a pretty garnish. For sandwiches mix the sardines with mayonnaise and spread upon thin slices of bread and butter.

BUCKWHEAT CAKES.

Mix together one cup of buckwheat flour, half an even teaspoonful of salt, one cupful of lukewarm water, and one eighth of a yeast-cake dissolved in three extra tablespoonfuls of water. Set to rise over night. Just before breakfast add one teaspoonful of New Orleans molasses and three tablespoonfuls of hot water in which has been dissolved one eighth of a teaspoonful of soda, and beat together well.

One or two spoonfuls of the batter may be saved from the batch to add to the next mixing.

This gives a pleasing acidity to the cakes.

Buckwheat may be eaten from October until April; it is too heating during the rest of the year.

Properly made, buckwheat cakes are nutritious and have great "staying" qualities; they are to Americans what oatmeal is to the Scotch. Grease griddle delicately with olive-oil.

MILK BREAD (TWO LOAVES).

Between five and six o'clock in the afternoon make a sponge in the following way:

Pour one and a half cupfuls of boiling water on six hops and when just lukewarm, strain, squeezing the hops dry.

Measure this water and add enough more water to make an exact cup and a half. Melt in this hop-water half a cake of yeast and add three even cupfuls of flour dipped from the bag and sifted after measuring. Use a three-quart basin; cover closely, and set in a warm place until about nine o'clock, when the sponge should fill the basin about two thirds full or a little over. Measure and sift three more cupfuls of flour, add one heaping teaspoonful of salt and a pinch over, and put into a six-quart vessel (agate or earthenware). Add a heaping teaspoonful of lard and one tablespoonful of sugar, and mix. Then pour in the sponge; rinse out the basin with one and a half cupfuls of rich, creamy milk, even measure; add this to the flour, and mix. Turn on a lightly floured board and knead into a soft springy mass, using an even half-cupful, or less, of flour (according to its compactness) for this purpose. More flour will make the bread hard.

Put it back into the large basin; cover closely and raise all night in a temperature of about 68° or 70°.

By seven in the morning or a little earlier, it should nearly or quite fill the basin. Turn out and knead just long enough to form into loaves. Use not more than a teaspoonful of flour for this last kneading, as the dough must be soft and elastic.

Put into pans; prick all over with a fork and raise, covered, an hour or two in about 90° of heat, when the dough should have more than doubled in size.

For the first ten minutes the oven should be hot enough to lightly brown the top; at the end of this time, moderate the fire a little, or place the bread in a cooler part of the oven, and continue to bake for thirty-five minutes longer. Use new milk when possible, otherwise scald and cool. In hot weather use it cold; in cold weather, lukewarm.

In cold weather set the dough on a feather cushion while it is rising, and cover with a woollen blanket at night.

This bread is not at its best the day it is baked. It will keep a week properly protected from the air in an earthen crock, and should be entirely cold before being put away.

Use the square-cornered bread pans, filling each a little less than half full: when the dough rises to the top, it is ready for the oven.

Flour varies in degree of compactness from one time to another, owing to certain conditions, so that a cupful from one bag will measure when sifted, more than a cupful from another bag of the same brand when that is sifted. Only experience and practice can teach one how to regulate and overcome these variations. Wheat grown at different seasons yields a different quality of flour. Its age after grinding has something to do with its quality; also a humid climate.

When bread and cake deteriorate after the middle of the barrel is passed, the cause will sometimes be found to be dampness. Drying the flour in the oven, sifting and cooling it, will in all probability improve it greatly.

Flour should always be kept in a cool, dry place: a bag may stand on a shelf, but a barrel should be set on a raised frame of slats, for it surely will become damp if allowed to rest upon the basement floor.

Flour of a very compact nature will require more wetting in the sponge.

When mixing, if the sponge is stiff and flaky instead of smooth and moist, add a spoonful or two of lukewarm water, sprinkling it on and stirring it in.

Too much moisture will make bread tough and flabby, and it will make cake heavy; on the other hand, too much flour will make bread stiff and cake "floury."

When of an unusually compact quality, try sifting before measuring, for cake.

Some cake-makers have better success by greasing only the bottom of the pans, cutting the cake from the sides after it becomes cold.

Cake should be put into a moderate oven at first, the heat being increased towards the last.

This allows the batter to expand before the cake browns.

Pastry flour is preferred by some people for cake and pastry; this is made from winter wheat.

Flour made from spring wheat is considered best for bread.

Spring-wheat flour generally requires more moisture than winter-wheat flour.

If by adding extra wetting, by sifting or heating, flour still yields unsatisfactory results, mix with one or two cups of pastry flour, which will give bread of lighter texture.

GLUTEN BREAD.

Six cups entire-wheat flour, three cups of water, half a yeast-cake, one teaspoonful of salt, two tablespoonfuls New Orleans molasses.

Make a sponge between six and seven P. M.

of one half the flour, half the water, and the yeast. At nine o'clock, or thereabouts, add the remainder of the water and flour, the salt and molasses, and knead with one half cup extra of flour, into a smooth, soft mass.

Set to rise until morning, then make into two loaves, let rise again to double the size, and bake in a moderate oven about fifty minutes.

HOME-MADE YEAST.

Put into a small preserving jar half a cake of yeast, and add one cupful of lukewarm water in which potatoes have been boiled (unsalted), and two even tablespoonfuls of sugar; let stand covered in a warm place, (about 90°), to ferment for three hours.

Half of this yeast is equal to half a yeast-cake, and in a cold place will keep sweet for a week.

When any yeast is taken out replace it (three hours before using) with potato-water and *one* spoonful of sugar, and allow it to ferment, as at first directed.

If at the end of a week none has been taken out, pour off one half and replace with potato-water and sugar. Always stir well before taking any out, and in making bread use a half-cupful less of water on the hops.

This yeast may be kept alive indefinitely if

the potato-water and sugar are added at the right time (three hours before using), and the other directions are observed. After the first week the yeast should be used directly after fermenting or the bread may be sour.

It should be renewed at least every seventh day. It can, however, be made daily if one requires yeast so often. If potato-water is not at hand pour a half-cupful of boiling water upon one tablespoonful of scraped raw potato, and use this when lukewarm.

POTTED MEATS.

Remove bones, fat, and gristle, from any cold pot-roast of veal, lamb, or poultry, and pound to a paste in a mortar (or use chopping-bowl and potato-masher). Add spice, or any of the seasoning sauces to taste, or season simply with salt and cayenne pepper. Put into an earthen dish and steam in the steamer for two or three hours. Meanwhile, cover the bones (broken if poultry) with water, and boil down to a glaze. Add this to the pounded meat with a teaspoonful of melted butter for each half-cupful of meat. Pack into small jars, holding enough for one occasion, and bake in a slow oven half an hour. When cold, pour over each jar a quarter of an inch of melted butter, and set away in a cold place. Boiled ham or tongue will need no salt. Scraps may be used for potting.

CLAM FRITTERS.

If the soft-shell clams are used, they must be washed several times in their own liquor, with a little water added to free them from sand, straining the liquor each time.

The rule for the batter is given in Fruit Fritters, and will require one pint of clams chopped in the chopping bowl. Leave out the salt and substitute a little of the clam-juice for the milk.

CUCUMBERS SERVED WITH CREAM.

Peel, slice very thin, and soak for an hour in ice-water, one cucumber and one onion.

Drain, arrange in salad-bowl, add salt and pepper to taste, and pour on sweet cream which has had a sufficient quantity of cider vinegar stirred into it to make it agreeably sour. Add a pinch of salt. Serve with the main part of the meal. This is a delicious dish, and it is claimed that the cream makes the cucumbers digestible.

SPICED FISH (SOMETIMES CALLED SOUSED OR POTTED FISH).

Whitefish, bass, shad, or mackerel may be used. Cut the raw fish into pieces suitable in size to serve as a portion. Put them in layers with salt, peppercorns, two or three whole cloves, and a little cinnamon stick, into an earthen jar, cover with cider vinegar, and bake covered in a very slow oven for about eight hours. Keep in a dry, cool place.

Serve for luncheon or tea. The cloves and cinnamon can be omitted if desired.

BIRDS.

It is a good plan to vary the monotony of every-day fare, by having a bird for dinner as often as once a week—chicken, duck, squab, pigeon, partridge, grouse, etc., can all be had at certain times in their season at moderate cost, if one takes the trouble to study the market. All of these birds make delicious fricassees, or they can be roasted in the oven, broiled or smothered, or be made into pies. The scraps can be made into croquettes for the next day's dinner, or potted for sandwiches. The rules given for preparing and cooking chicken and duck may be applied to game birds.

A half-cupful of meat minced fine in chopping-bowl, after discarding all bone, gristle, and fat, will make two croquettes. Add salt and pepper to taste, and enough gravy (thickened with flour), to mould into egg-shaped rolls. Sprinkle liberally with powdered bread crumbs, and brown in a teaspoonful of hot butter in an uncovered frying-pan. If covered they will fall to pieces. If no gravy is at hand with which to bind the meat together, make a thick drawn-butter and use that instead. Serve with a spoonful of bread-sauce made as follows : Soak one teaspoonful of rolled bread crumbs in one fourth of a cupful of boiling water; add this to the butter left in the pan, after removing the croquettes, and boil until thick enough to spread evenly. Add any seasoning sauce, onion-, lemon-juice, or beef extract. Send to table with a sprig of celery or watercress, on each croquette. Croquettes may be made the day before they are needed and kept in the ice-box. Bread them just before frying.

CHOCOLATE CUSTARD FOR LAYER CAKE.

Two squares of chocolate, one half-cup of granulated sugar, one half-cup of rich milk, one rounded tablespoonful of flour, one half of an egg, one pinch of salt, one half-teaspoonful of vanilla. Stir the flour, salt, sugar, and chocolate broken into bits, together; add the egg and three spoonfuls of the milk; stir, and set over hot water, stirring until the chocolate is melted. Then add slowly the rest of the milk; stand the saucepan on the stove and cook gently for a few minutes, being careful not to scorch, and stir constantly. It should be jelly-like but not stiff; take from the fire, add vanilla, and when a little cool spread on the cakes. Frost the top layer, or dust on powdered sugar.

INDIAN MUFFINS.

Two heaping cupfuls of flour, one heaping cupful of yellow corn-meal, one half-cupful of butter (scant), one even cupful of sugar, three eggs, two cupfuls of milk, three teaspoonfuls of baking powder, one half level teaspoonful of salt. Sift together thoroughly the flour meal, salt, and powder. Beat the eggs and sugar, and stir in the milk; add this to the flour, etc., and at the last add the butter, melted. Bake in the deep muffin-pans in a moderately hot oven; serve hot. Warm up by standing in a steamer on a plate.

SOUSE (PICKLED PIGS' FEET).

The butcher will send the feet parboiled. Brush and scrape them with scrupulous care, and boil in enough boiling water to cover for five or six hours, replenishing from the boiling teakettle as needed. Pigs' feet must be cooked very tender, almost jelly-like, but not so long that they will fall to pieces. When done, sprinkle all sides with salt (after taking them from the pot) and put them in an earthen jar. Add cayenne pepper, a few peppercorns, cloves, cinnamon, a bay leaf, and enough boiling cider vinegar to cover. In a cold place, souse will keep a month or longer. Warm up in the chafing-dish or frying-pan. Serve with lettuce or watercress sandwiches. Souse makes a relishable little after-theatre supper.

SAUSAGE MEAT.

Three fourths of a pound of lean, and one fourth of a pound of fat pork, one level teaspoonful of salt, one rounded teaspoonful of finely powdered sage ; add one half-teaspoonful of black pepper. Chop the pork very fine, or grind it, distribute the salt, etc., evenly through the meat and pack in an earthen dish. It will be ready to use in a day. In cold weather several pounds may be made up at one time ; pour melted (not hot) lard over the top to exclude the air ; cover closely and keep in a cold, even temperature. Corn-fed young pork makes the most delicious sausage. Home-dried sage is the best and most savory to use.

TOMATO FRITTERS.

Skin and slice cold, ripe tomatoes ; pepper and salt lightly, and dip each slice into a batter made of equal parts of milk, melted butter, and flour. Fry in a frying-pan, turn with a cake-turner so as not to break, and after browning one side cook slowly.

Time, about twenty minutes.

If preferred the tomatoes may be breaded and then fried in hot butter.

CORN BREAD.

One generous tablespoonful of butter, one fourth cup of sugar, and two eggs creamed together; one and a half cupfuls of milk, two cupfuls of flour, one cupful of yellow Indian meal, three teaspoonfuls baking-powder, and an even half-teaspoonful of salt. Bake in a moderate oven, in a bread pan. Serve hot the first meal.

SPONGE CAKE.

Four eggs, one cup of granulated sugar, three quarters of a cup of sifted flour, two pinches of salt, juice and grated rind of half a lemon. Whisk the yolks until thick and foaming, which will take some ten minutes. Add the sugar and grated lemon-rind and beat (always beating—never stirring), for ten minutes longer; add the whisked whites, beating them in lightly; then sift in the flour and fold together lightly, then add the lemon-juice, beating as delicately as possible, and bake immediately, either in the deep sponge-cake pan, or the deep muffin-pans, for about twenty minutes, in a rather quick oven. To measure the flour for this cake it must be sifted into the measure, the salt added, and then sifted eight or nine times more. No baking-powder is required, for if put together as directed, it will be light enough. The whites of eggs for cake should be beaten only long enough to make a coarse light froth, and beating should cease the moment that they are stiff. For méringues, they can be beaten a little longer; too much beating toughens them.

SPAGHETTI WITH TOMATO SAUCE.

Spaghetti is the small pipe macaroni. It can be cooked *au gratin* (that is, baked with cheese), or served buttered with grated cheese passed, or with a rich tomato-sauce as follows: Into a quart of fast-boiling water put a cupful of spaghetti broken into pieces; add half a teaspoonful of salt, and boil for several minutes, stirring to keep the pieces separated.

Cover and stand the pot where it will keep just below the boiling point, for twenty minutes; then bring forward and boil steadily for about thirty-five minutes.

It must cook just long enough to mash easily. Too long cooking will destroy its nutritive qualities. The cover may be left partly off during the last half-hour, so that the water may cook away, thus avoiding the necessity for draining. Macaroni is sweeter not to be drained. To make the sauce, put into another saucepan a slice of onion, a clove, and a sprig of parsley or celery. Add a heaping tablespoonful of butter and fry delicately; add a tablespoonful of flour, and stir until a pale brown; then add two cupfuls of cooked and strained tomatoes. Cook a few minutes; remove the onion, clove, and parsley; add the spaghetti. Salt, and pepper to taste, and serve hot. Macaroni may be warmed up by setting the dish covered in a place where it will heat but not cook. It may have bouillon added and make a delicious soup. It may have milk and a little soda added, making a tomato bisque.

FANCY DESSERTS.

STRAWBERRY WHIP.

Mash to a pulp one cupful of ripe strawberries, and sweeten to taste. Add one teaspoonful of gelatine soaked in a tablespoonful of cold water and then melted; also the white of an egg whisked to a froth. Set on ice, and serve ice cold in champagne glasses. Pass ladyfingers.

Cherries or raspberries may be served in the same way.

A teaspoonful of whipped cream to each portion is a great addition.

COFFEE BAVARIAN CREAM.

Soak for half an hour one heaping tablespoonful of gelatine, in one quarter of a cupful of milk. Beat until very creamy (in an agate saucepan) the yolk of one egg, and two heaping tablespoonfuls of granulated sugar, and pour on this slowly, stirring continually, two thirds of a cupful of milk, boiling hot. Set into another saucepan containing boiling water, and cook four minutes, stirring constantly from the bottom and sides.

Then add the soaked gelatine, stir and cook one minute longer, and add a pinch of salt.

When cold, and before it is set, add half a cupful of cold, strong coffee. (Java is best.)

As soon as the coffee is well stirred in, whip in the cream, which is prepared in this way.

Whip to a stiff froth five tablespoonfuls of cream; add the white of the egg whisked to a stiff froth, then add the coffee and pour into a shallow glass dish. Set in a cold, but not freezing place for several hours: in summer set on ice. When thoroughly set, add the Sea-foam cream, flavored with two teaspoonfuls of coffee.

To be a success the quantities must be measured very carefully; it is a delicious dish when made just right.

Five *even* teaspoonfuls of gelatine will make the one heaping tablespoonful required.

Two heaping dessert-spoonfuls of coffee in two thirds of a cupful of boiling water will make the coffee.

To get a level teaspoonful of gelatine, press down with a broad knife-blade.

CARAMEL SEA-FOAM CREAM MOUSSE.

Sea-foam cream is made of whipped cream and whipped gelatine, and it cannot be a success unless both will whip perfectly. The cream must be stiff, and the gelatine a solid froth before they are put together.

Put one cupful of ice-cold cream and two teaspoonfuls of caramel into a cold bowl set in another of cracked ice and salt.

Whip until stiff; then add three tablespoonfuls of confectioner's sugar, a few drops of extract of vanilla, and a few grains of salt.

Soak four level teaspoonfuls of gelatine in twenty teaspoonfuls of cold water ten minutes.

Then melt over the teakettle, and when a little cool whip until it is a solid froth, which will take about ten minutes.

Add this to the cream, and whip all together thoroughly; turn into a cold mould, and pack in ice and salt for three hours.

When ready to serve, turn out on a cold dish, and serve with any seasonable fruit, such as berries, or oranges cut in slices. Ripe peaches may be peeled and halved, the stone-cavities filled with cracked ice, and covered with sugar; half a fine peach is a portion. The fruit should be chilled. Care should be taken to have all utensils perfectly dry and clean, as gelatine will not whip to a froth if salt, cream, white of egg, or any foreign substance touches it before frothing.

Cream sold in half-pint glass jars is reliable for whipping.

SEA-FOAM CREAM FOR PUDDINGS.

Whip to a stiff froth four tablespoonfuls of cream; add two teaspoonfuls of confectioner's sugar and a few grains of salt.

Soak one level teaspoonful of gelatine in four teaspoonfuls of cold water ten minutes; then melt over the teakettle or in the oven.

When a little cool, whip with a wire spoon six or seven minutes; it should be well frothed at the end of this time. Add immediately to the whipped cream, and beat well for a minute or two; flavor with vanilla, wine, coffee, or caramel, according to the dish it is to be used on.

Pour on the cold pudding or cake, and set on ice for an hour or two.

BOILED RICE WITH WHIPPED-EGG SAUCE.

Wash, but do not soak, a scant half-cupful of rice (Carolina rice is best). Pour this into two cupfuls of milk, stirring until it boils; then add an even half-teaspoonful of salt, cover closely, and boil very slowly for half an hour on a cool part of the stove. Serve hot, either with whipped-egg sauce, or with butter and sugar, or cream and sugar, or with tutti-frutti sauce.

TUTTI-FRUTTI SAUCE FOR PLAIN PUDDINGS.

Seed half a cupful of table raisins, pour over them a cupful of cold water, and set on the stove to get hot gradually. Simmer half an hour; then add a teaspoonful each of candied citron, orange, and lemon peel, chopped fine; also, if desired, a few blanched almonds, also chopped, and one third of a cupful of sugar; simmer until the candied fruit is soft enough to break when pressed between the fingers. Thicken with one level teaspoonful of cornstarch blended with one heaping teaspoonful of butter. Add brandy or wine.

If the water boils away, add more from the boiling kettle.

SAUCE FOR STRAWBERRY SHORTCAKE.

Beat together one tablespoonful of butter and two of sugar. Add the yolk of an egg and beat several minutes; then whisk in the frothed white and one third of a cupful of boiling water.

Cook over the teakettle about two minutes, and add any part of or the whole of a cup of cream.

Keep hot, but do not cook.

Heat the cream before adding it to the egg mixture. Salt to taste and flavor with a tablespoonful of sherry.

FRUIT FRITTERS: PEACHES, APPLES, OR BERRIES.

One half-cupful flour, one third cupful milk, one half-teaspoonful baking-powder, one egg, a large pinch of salt, one dessert-spoonful of melted butter, one pint of sliced fruit or berries or stoned cherries.

Sift flour, baking-powder and salt together; beat the egg; add the butter and milk, then the flour, and lastly the fruit, lightly sugared if desired.

Bake in spoonfuls on a griddle.

Serve hot, either with butter and powdered sugar or hot sugar syrup, (one cup of sugar cooked until clear with one third of a cup of water). Corn fritters may be made of this rule by adding a pint of grated or chopped corn to the batter.

MUSKMELONS WITH ICE-CREAM AND FRUIT.

Put small muskmelons on ice, and just before serving, cut in halves, remove the seeds, and serve with a spoonful of ice-cream in each half.

Ice-cold whipped cream may be used in place of ice-cream. Flavor and sweeten to taste.

If Sea-foam cream is preferred, set the melons on ice for an hour or two before and after putting in the cream.

If muskmelons are not sweet and delicious, cut them into cubes (of course rejecting the rind) and serve slightly salted with sweetened cream, or cream and powdered sugar. Melons that would be disappointing by themselves, are excellent when served with well sugared fruit.

A single variety of fruit may be used, or a mixture of berries and cherries, pineapple, peaches, plums, grapes and orange juice in the following way: Shred the pineapple, peel and quarter the peaches, quarter and stone the plums and seed the grapes.

Mix together, add a little orange juice and some brandy or Jamaica rum, and when it is ice cold arrange in small melon-halves, one for each portion.

Sugar to taste.

LUNCHEON DESSERT. FRENCH TOAST WITH SUGAR, SYRUP, OR HONEY.

Beat an egg with a gill of milk; add salt to taste; dip slices of bread, or the steamed raised dumpling in this batter, and fry a delicate brown in hot butter.

Melt one cupful of sugar with half a cupful of water, cook a few minutes, flavor with lemon extract, brandy, or fruit syrup, and serve hot.

FRUIT CAKE.

Sift together one teaspoonful each of nutmeg, allspice, cloves, salt, two teaspoonfuls cinnamon, three cups flour, and one heaping teaspoonful of baking powder.

Add to this one pound of currants, one pound of raisins, seeded, and half a pound of citron sliced fine.

Beat two eggs into one cup of molasses, cream one cup of butter with one cup of brown sugar; add to the molasses; beat well; add one cupful of strong coffee, and then the flour, etc. Bake two and a half hours in a slow oven, careful not to let it burn.

In a close tin box, this cake has been kept for three years.

GOLD AND SILVER CAKE WITH OR WITHOUT FRUIT.

Use the rule for loaf cake as to quantities, beating, etc., for each cake excepting the eggs. The three eggs will do for the two cakes; the yolks for the gold cake, and the whites for the silver cake.

Add two tablespoonfuls of water to the gold cake and if desired two cupfuls of seeded raisins well floured.

Citron is the proper fruit for silver cake.

Slice half a pound in thin slices and add

about two tablespoonfuls of flour. (No extra flour will be needed if the citron is not used.)

Flavor with a few drops of almond extract.

Sometimes fruit is found to be more evenly distributed if it is put in the pan in alternate layers with the batter.

Citron cake will keep a month or longer.

POUND CAKE.

Three eighths of a cupful of butter, one cupful of flour, put lightly into the cup, one slightly rounded teaspoonful of baking-powder, a large pinch of salt, one half-cupful of granulated sugar, two eggs, one teaspoonful of brandy or other flavoring.

With the hand cream the butter; add the flour (sifted three times with salt and powder) and stir until light, (it should look like whipped cream at this stage) then add the sugar and flavoring and stir for several minutes. Add the eggs (unbeaten) and beat (still with the hand) for two minutes longer.

Bake in a moderate oven about forty minutes.

MOLASSES CAKE.

Stir together in a mixing-bowl, half a cupful of Porto Rico molasses, half a cupful of darkest brown sugar, one third of a cupful of softened (not melted) butter, one egg, half a teaspoonful of cinnamon, the same of ginger, a pinch each of cloves, allspice, mace (or nutmeg) and salt.

Sift with one and a half cupfuls of flour, one teaspoonful of cream of tartar; add two cupfuls of raisins, which have been stoned and steamed (on a plate) for an hour in a steamer. Add one fourth of a cupful of warm water (in which has been dissolved one half of a level teaspoonful of soda), then add the flour and raisins. Stir lightly, but thoroughly, and pour into a shallow pan lined with greased paper and bake one hour in a moderate oven.

When a broom straw will come out free from dough, the cake is done.

GINGER SNAPS.

Stir together until thoroughly mixed, one cup either of butter or beef drippings, one cupful of molasses, one cupful brown sugar, pressed down, two heaping teaspoonfuls ground ginger, and half a level teaspoonful of soda, dissolved in four heaping tablespoonfuls of cold water. Add four cups of flour dipped from the bag, and sifted after measuring. Roll out an eighth of an inch in thickness and cut with a $2\frac{1}{2}$-inch cutter. Lift with a broad knife-blade or cake-turner, and arrange on the inverted bottom of buttered tins; bake in a moderate hot oven, very careful not to burn. If butter or the fat from corned beef is used, a pinch of salt will be required, but with lard or beef drippings salt to taste.

Porto Rico molasses makes a dark colored snap and it is preferred on this account as well as for its flavor by some cooks.

New Orleans molasses, on the other hand, has a yellow hue and is more delicate in flavor. Mash the soda very fine and smooth off with a knife-blade; then divide exactly in the middle, lengthwise of the spoon.

Flour the board and rolling-pin and only roll out about one eighth of the quantity at a time. Put the trimmings aside and roll out by themselves at the last. Use as little flour as possible in rolling out. This quantity will make one hundred snaps. Keep in air-tight glass jars in a dry place.

HOT GINGERBREAD AND WAFERS.

Mix together half a cupful of butter (softened but not melted) two thirds of a cupful of New Orleans molasses, three tablespoonfuls of cold water in which has been dissolved one third of a level teaspoonful of soda (mashed before measuring) and one teaspoonful of ground ginger.

Add one heaping cupful of flour dipped from the bag and sifted after measuring, with a pinch of salt.

Stir till smooth and pour one half of the batter into a very shallow pan; bake in a hot oven and serve hot, breaking into portions instead of cutting.

Put the remainder of the batter in half teaspoonfuls (two inches apart) upon the bottom of inverted tins lightly buttered, and bake in a quick oven.

These wafers are crisp when fresh; if they become soft, set them in a hot oven for a few minutes and when cold they will be crisp again.

Served hot, with cream for sauce, gingerbread makes a very nice dessert.

SOFT GINGERBREAD. (HOT OR COLD.)

One cup of molasses, one half-cup butter, one fourth of a cup of warm water, one level teaspoonful of soda, two teaspoonfuls of ginger, one egg, two cups of sifted flour.

Stir the soda into the molasses until it foams, beat in the egg, add the butter (softened but not melted) then the water, ginger and flour.

Bake in a shallow tin about thirty minutes in a moderate oven.

Put the flour lightly in the cup when measuring, as too much flour will spoil the cake.

A pinch of salt may be added. If the taste of soda is objected to, add half a teaspoonful of cream of tartar to the flour.

FONDANT, OR FOUNDATION FOR CREAM CANDIES.

Stir while dissolving on the edge of the stove, two cupfuls of granulated sugar, one cupful of water, a few grains of salt, and a big pinch of cream of tartar; then boil gently without further stirring.

Wipe away any crystals that form above the edge of the syrup while boiling, but do not touch the syrup or jar it, or it will grain. Use for the purpose a sharp stick with a piece of wet muslin upon it.

Boil, not too vigorously, fifteen minutes, then dip a smooth stick into ice-water, then into the syrup, and back again into the ice-water. If the syrup thickly adhering to the stick will become like soft putty when worked between the thumb and finger, it is ready to turn out. Keep on testing every minute until this stage is reached, then turn it out into a deep and rather flaring earthen bowl, lightly oiled or buttered.

Let it cool a few minutes, and when the finger-tip pressed gently, will dent it, stir (before a crust forms) round and round with a stout wooden spoon, until it becomes a snow-white creamy mass.

Put in the flavoring while stirring: a half-teaspoonful each of rose and vanilla is a good combination which blends well with nuts, chocolate, or candied fruit.

Kneading improves the fondant.

For sugar-plums, form the fondant around whole nut meats, dip into granulated sugar and shake violently in a bowl with a few additional spoonfuls of sugar: almonds are the nuts generally used for this candy.

An inch piece of the fondant with an English walnut meat on each side makes another variation.

For chocolate cream bar, melt one half-square of chocolate over the teakettle, and stir in a lump of fondant the size of an egg. A knife and fork facilitates this process.

Put a layer of plain fondant on either side, an inch in thickness and cover all over with a coat of melted chocolate (one square will be enough) flavored with a few drops of vanilla.

In a day, this may be cut into squares.

For nut bar, mix nuts with the fondant, press into a square, and in a day cut into small cubes. Candied fruit, candied orange peel, crystallized ginger, etc., may also be covered with fondant for sugar-plums.

If properly made, fondant will keep for months in air-tight glass jars and be improved in quality.

If the syrup boils a little too long, the fondant will not mass, but on being stirred will crumble when it reaches the snow-white stage. When this occurs a *few* drops of water or wine may be sprinkled over the surface and stirred in (a drop too much will spoil it).

Set the bowl in a basin of boiling water, boil and stir constantly until smooth. If the stirring is not kept up the fondant will turn into syrup. To be right it should be pliable enough to be moulded into any shape when it is cool enough to handle.

If the fondant grains from too much boiling or jarring of the syrup, a few spoonfuls of water may be added and a new trial made, melting, boiling and testing as before, or it may be melted into syrup for the table.

If the fondant after being creamed seems soft and gummy and does not retain its shape it has not been boiled quite long enough.

This condition is worse than the other.

To remedy it knead in confectioner's sugar, until it will take no more : the candies will be eatable, but that is all.

Vanilla and sherry make a fine flavor.

The novice in candy-making, would do well to try only a quarter of the quantities given, at first.

Begin testing after the sugar has been cooking ten minutes, for small quantities.

A dry atmosphere is desirable while boiling syrup for candies, and it is well to choose a fine bright day for the work.

Sarah E. Craig, in *20th Century Cookery*, says:

"I would suggest the sugar thermometer to those having trouble in testing their syrups for candy-making.

"One can be bought for $1.75, and will save the amateur a world of trouble. In making fondant the thermometer will register about 238⁰, and the syrup is then ready to turn out."

A very satisfactory cream can be easily made with confectioner's sugar, but it is not nearly so good as that just described.

Beat the white of an egg with a tablespoonful of water or cream, and stir in confectioner's sugar until enough has been added to form a pliable dough. Flavor while mixing.

Fruit juice or fruit syrups may be used instead of water or cream.

If preferred, the egg may be omitted.

MISCELLANEOUS RECIPES.

HOW TO MAKE COFFEE.

There are various ways of making coffee, and where one fails, others may be tried with success.

Some kinds of coffee are best when made by the French method, which consists in pouring boiling water on the finely ground coffee placed upon a set of strainers in a cylinder, and allowing it to percolate slowly through.

Another way is to mix the coffee with egg and cold water, and bring it to a boil; then settle, strain, and serve.

Yet another is to mix coffee and egg, add a little cold water, and then boiling water; bring to a boil; stand to settle; strain, and serve.

In all cases the pot should be tight as possible, to prevent the escape of the aroma, and the coffee should be served soon after being made.

An earthen pipkin makes a good coffee-pot: place a doubled cheese-cloth under the lid, and tuck it in closely. The cheese-cloth is to be used as a strainer, and it must be thoroughly washed and boiled every time it is used, and renewed often, as otherwise the flavor of the coffee would be spoiled.

Buy only the best grades of coffee, and when possible have it ground at home. A third each of Java, Mocha, and Maracaibo makes a favorite blend. Another is two thirds Java and one third Mocha.

To make one quart of coffee take one heaping cupful of coffee, one third of a raw egg, half a cupful of cold water, and one quart of boiling.

To make one cupful of coffee take two heaping dessert-spoonfuls of coffee, two spoonfuls of cold water, one teaspoonful of raw egg, and one cupful of boiling water.

Too much egg will weaken the coffee.

MINCE-MEAT.

Five pounds of cooked beef. After the meat is chopped, measure it in a bowl, and to each bowl of meat add two bowls of chopped apples and one of chopped raisins; mix these together, and set aside.

Chop a pound of suet fine, add one heaping tablespoonful of salt, the same each of cinnamon and allspice, two tablepoonfuls of clove, two nutmegs, and not quite a tablespoonful of mace. Add also one pound of sugar, a scant pint of molasses, and one quart of cider; put these ingredients in a kettle, and let them come to a boil; this melts the sugar and suet and mixes the spices.

Take from the fire, and when cool add to the meat, apples and raisins, and stir in, finally, half a pint of whiskey. The sugar, salt, and spices may be varied to suit the individual taste.

CANDIED ORANGE PEEL.

Soak the orange peel in a brine strong enough to float a potato, for several days; then steep in cold water until it is so tender that it can be broken easily under slight pressure. The water should be changed six or eight times in order to make the flavor of the peel more delicate. Drain for several hours; then cut it into inch squares; measure, and put it on the back part of the stove, with an equal amount of granulated sugar. When thoroughly dissolved, spread upon platters, and keep in the open oven or in the sunshine until candied, which will be in a few days. Pack away in covered glass jars.

Lemon peel may be prepared in the same way.

CANNED PEACHES.

Allow one pint of water and one cupful of sugar for every quart of peaches. Boil sugar and water for ten minutes; then add the peaches (peeled, but not stoned), a few at a time, and boil until a broom-straw will pierce them easily; be sure to have them cooked enough.

Put the peaches in jars (two thirds full), boil,

and skim the syrup, and pour it over the peaches until the jars overflow.

Seal at once.

Use new rubbers each season, as old ones are apt to be unelastic. If there is not enough syrup for the last jar, make more of sugar and water; canned fruit is always improved by plenty of syrup. Keep canned goods in a cool, dry place, the darker the better.

PRESERVED PEACHES.

Select sound, ripe peaches of a fine, rich variety; peel, halve, and stone them.

Weigh, and make a syrup of an equal amount of granulated sugar.

To every three pounds of sugar add one cupful of water; melt, and boil ten minutes; then drop in the peaches and cook them until a broom-straw will pierce them easily.

Skim carefully.

Put the fruit in jars, boil and skim the syrup a few minutes longer, fill the jars to overflowing with the syrup, and seal.

A few stones may be boiled with the syrup, and two or three put in each jar to flavor.

This is the old-fashioned peach preserve of our grandmothers.

When serving, a teaspoonful of fine brandy may be added to the juice for each portion.

Peaches may be easily peeled by pouring

boiling water on them and allowing them to stand about a minute; a longer time would soften them too much. Scald only a half a dozen at a time.

Keep peeled fruit covered with a wet cloth to prevent discoloration.

When peeling with a knife, a good plan is to halve and stone them before peeling.

SPICED PEACHES.

Seven pounds of peaches, three and a half pounds of sugar, one scant pint of cider vinegar, half an ounce of stick cinnamon, half an ounce of whole cloves, half a teaspoonful of whole allspice, and one quarter of a nutmeg broken into bits.

Make a syrup by boiling the sugar and vinegar together about ten minutes. Put in enough peeled peaches to cover the bottom of the kettle and cook gently and steadily until a broomstraw will pierce them easily. Skim the peaches out carefully; put them on a platter and cook the remainder of the fruit in the same way.

When all are done, drain off the juice, put it in the kettle, boil up, and skim off the froth.

Put the peaches in a stone jar, pour the hot syrup over them, tie the spices in a bag and lay it on top; cover closely, and at the end of a week pour off the juice, boil up, and pour it hot over the peaches.

If the vinegar is too sharp, a few spoonfuls of water may be added. If preferred a few of the cloves may be stuck in the peaches before boiling.

Some cooks prefer to leave the skins on peaches put up this way, considering them richer. Use late fruit and select only the best and largest.

The bag for spices should be of very coarse muslin and must be large enough to cover the top.

Keep in a cool, dry place where the temperature is even.

QUINCES.

Wash, peel, and cut into slices an inch thick; remove the cores and cook until very tender in water. Skim out the fruit and set aside.

Add sugar to the water; boil and skim; return the quinces to this syrup; boil up and seal at once in glass jars.

Pour water on the seeds and skins, boil and strain and add sugar; this makes a very good jelly.

Follow the rule for crab-apple jelly.

For quince preserves use a pound of sugar to one of fruit.

PRESERVED PINEAPPLE.

Make a syrup of one pint of sugar and half a

cupful of water ; boil until clear, and add a pint of pineapple which has been peeled, sliced, and cored.

Cook fifteen minutes.

Put in glass jars, and when cold tie the jars up in thick brown paper to exclude the light.

CANNED CHERRIES.

One quart of fine large cherries, three heaping tablespoonfuls granulated sugar and four tablespoonfuls of water.

Boil water and sugar until clear; add the cherries which have been stemmed, washed, and drained, and cook them, covered, ten minutes. Seal in pint jars.

More sugar will make a richer preserve.

Prepared in this way cherries are very nice for steamed puddings, but they may also be used as a sauce by adding more sugar at the table.

In canning always fill the jars brimming full; let them stand a minute to settle; then add more juice and seal, hot.

PLUMS. (DAMSON OR LARGE BLUE VARIETY). STEWED OR FOR CANNING.

Wipe the plums with a soft cloth : use the firmest for preserving, the others for stewing.

Measure, and allow nearly an equal amount

of granulated sugar and the same of water. Cook sugar and water ten minutes after it boils clear.

Add the fruit and cook several minutes or until a broom straw will pierce easily. A heaping pint of plums will take a scant pint of sugar, and an even pint of water. Seal hot in air-tight glass jars.

Plum juice diluted to taste with water and cracked ice makes a delicious and refreshing drink.

GRAPE PRESERVES.

Use Catawba grapes and pulp them.

Measure the skins and allow as much sugar as there are skins, and the same amount of water.

Put half of the sugar in the oven to get hot, and put the other half in a kettle with the water; boil until clear and add the skins, a few at a time, so that the syrup may not stop boiling.

Keep the pot covered, and do not stir, as stirring will cause the skins to lose their plumpness and become tough.

Shaking the pot occasionally will prevent burning. It will take a quart of skins about half an hour to cook.

Cook the pulps about ten minutes to loosen the seeds, and when cool enough, strain closely through a piece of cheese-cloth. Put back over the fire, boil and skim; then add to the skins, stir, add the hot sugar, boil a minute or two, and put away in glasses the same as jelly.

In cooking syrup or anything that needs skimming let the vessel boil only on one side; the froth will then be thrown to the opposite side and may be easily removed.

PRESERVED CITRON.

Cut citron in halves; turn the cut side down and slice with a broad, strong knife in slices a little more than an inch wide.

Peel, seed, and cut into inch-size pieces.

Soak over night in cold water (a quart of water to every quart of fruit, with a lump of alum the size of a large pea dissolved in each quart of water). Next morning rinse the citron in salted water (a teaspoonful of salt to a quart of water), and cook forty minutes in fresh warm water, (a quart of water to one of citron).

Meanwhile, make a syrup of six pounds of sugar and a pint of water in which two ounces of scraped and sliced ginger root has been boiled.

The ginger may be soaked first for half an hour or so in cold water to make it scrape more easily. Slice, and pour on it three cups of cold water, bring slowly to a boil and use two cups (one pint) for the syrup, throwing away the remainder.

Boil the syrup about ten minutes, tie half an

ounce of cinnamon stick, one teaspoonful of whole cloves, and half a teaspoonful of whole allspice in a piece of net or cheese-cloth and cook this in the syrup. Add the citron after draining and cook slowly half an hour.

Skim out and put in a stone jar.

Add to the syrup two thinly sliced lemons which have been cooked fifteen minutes in half a cupful of cold water (use water and all) and boil and skim for half an hour; then pour over the citron.

The spices and ginger root may be added also if preferred.

Keep in a cold place. When cold add one fine orange thinly sliced.

The following is the exact proportion of ingredients :

Six pounds of cut-up citron, six pounds of granulated sugar, one pint of water, alum size of a pea for each quart of citron, two ounces ginger root, two lemons, half a cupful of water, one half an ounce of stick cinnamon, one teaspoonful whole cloves, one half-teaspoonful allspice, one orange.

CRAB-APPLE JELLY.

Cover the apples with cold water and cook slowly until they are as soft as mush, then drain through a cloth laid over a sieve; do not press the fruit in the least.

Put the juice on the fire and cook a few minutes; then add an equal amount of sugar; boil and skim and put away in tumblers.

As apples yield a different quality of juice at different seasons, it is better to make up only a quart at first, and this will serve as a guide for the rest of the jelly, how long to boil, and how much water and sugar will be needed.

GRAPE JELLY.

Use Concord grapes; stem them, and keep them at the boiling-point in an agate saucepan (uncovered) on the back of the stove for four hours (stirring occasionally), to evaporate and get soft.

Mash with a wooden potato-masher, and stir with a wooden spoon.

Boil gently for another hour, or until the seeds drop out, careful not to let them burn. Stir often.

When cool enough, strain, a cupful at a time, through a piece of new canton-flannel wrung out of cold water. Measure the juice with exactness, and put an equal amount of granulated sugar on pans or platters in the oven, to get very hot, but not to melt, stirring occasionally.

While the sugar is heating, cook the juice in a clean agate saucepan, uncovered, half an hour.

Do not stir, but skim at the end of each fifteen minutes. Now add the hot sugar, and stir with a wooden spoon until it is all dissolved; then boil gently five minutes without stirring; skim; boil again for five minutes; skim again, and it is ready to put in glasses.

Put a silver teaspoon in each glass, and fill to the top; remove the spoon at once, as metal of any kind will discolor the jelly.

Put the jelly away, uncovered, for a day in a dry place, or in the sunshine; then cover with rounds of writing-paper dipped in brandy or alcohol, and tie over this rounds of paper.

Allow no water to touch the grapes; do not wash them, and see that all utensils are perfectly dry and clean.

If the foregoing directions are followed exactly, the jelly will be clear and rich in color, and of a perfect consistency. Keep in a dry, cool closet.

CURRANT JELLY.

Put the currants, unstemmed and unwashed, in an agate kettle. Heat, and mash with a wooden pestle, or spoon, and cook gently for fifteen minutes after boiling begins.

When cool enough not to burn the hand, strain, a cupful at a time, through a piece of stout cloth wrung very dry from hot water; press out every bit of juice.

Measure, and put an equal amount of granulated sugar in the oven to get very hot. Boil the juice for fifteen minutes slowly; skim; then stir in the hot sugar; boil ten or twelve minutes, and put into tumblers. One quart of currants will make two tumblers of jelly. Let no water touch the fruit during the process.

SYRUP FROM BERRIES.

Put very ripe perfect berries in an earthenware pot; mash, and let them stand over night in a warm room. Next day heat, but do not boil; strain through a cloth; measure; add an equal amount of granulated sugar; set on the stove, and stir until the sugar is dissolved, but do not cook; then seal hot in small, air-tight glass jars.

This syrup may be used for flavoring jellies or punches, or for making sherbets.

UNFERMENTED GRAPE-JUICE.

Ten cupfuls Concord grapes, six cupfuls water, two cupfuls sugar. Mash the grapes, and cook in three cupfuls of the water; strain; add to the skins and seeds three more cupfuls of water; cook again; strain; add to the strained juice the two cupfuls of sugar, and boil five minutes.

Skim, and bottle, hot, in air-tight jars.

In serving, add sugar and a little lemon-juice (or thin slices of lemon); fill glasses half full of cracked ice; pour in the grape juice, and a simple but delicious drink is the result.

LEMONADE.

Ten tablespoonfuls lemon-juice; ten heaping tablespoonfuls granulated sugar; one orange, sliced very thin; two even quarts of ice-water.

LEMON EXTRACT.

Cut the yellow rind from six fine large lemons, as thinly as possible, and cover with three fourths of a pint of best alcohol. Put in a wide-mouthed bottle and cork tightly. It will be ready for use in a few days.

EXTRACT OF VANILLA.

Break one vanilla-bean into inch pieces; cover with cold water and let it stand in a tightly corked bottle four days.

Then add half a pint of the best alcohol: it will be ready for use in a week.

Turn this off into another bottle, and add to the vanilla-bean a little more than half a cupful of alcohol: this will be ready by the time the first extract is all used.

The bottles should have glass stoppers.

Vanilla-beans are long, thin pods which sell for twenty cents each and can only be found at the large stores dealing in fine groceries. It is a great advantage to make one's extract, as most of that which is sold is not made from vanilla-beans at all.

GREEN TOMATO PICKLE.

Four quarts of green tomatoes sliced in nearly inch-thick slices.

One quart of white onions, and six green peppers sliced thinly.

Put them with salt in layers in an earthen vessel to stand over night. Use a rounded half-cupful of fine table salt.

In the morning drain for an hour; then pour over them three scant pints of genuine cider vinegar; add half a cupful of granulated sugar, a tablespoonful of whole cloves, half an ounce of stick cinnamon and a few allspice tied in a bag.

Cook gently for half an hour after boiling begins, keeping the cover partly off. Just before removing from the fire add an ounce of mustard seed; stir lightly, so as not to break the pieces, with a wooden spoon, and put away in an earthen jar for a month in a cool place. At the end of this time put it again on the stove and boil up with a half-cupful of sugar (more or less according to taste), and seal hot in jars.

Remove the bag of spices before sealing, and add a red pepper pod if not peppery enough. Before filling a jar, place in it a spoon long enough to extend above the edge of it. This will prevent breaking if the jar is a perfect one.

PICKLED STRING-BEANS AND CUCUMBERS.

Put one quart of young fresh string-beans into a brine which will float an egg.

At the end of three days take them out and put into the brine two dozen very small white onions. Wash the beans in ice-water and pour over them one pint of boiling cider vinegar in which is dissolved a lump of alum the size of a large pea.

In three days drain; steam the beans for twelve minutes in a steamer; then put them into a stone jar; add the onions, one small red pepper pod, one ounce of mixed whole spices tied in a bag, and pour over one pint of cider vinegar, boiling hot. Place a weight on the pickles to keep them submerged.

Throw away the brine and alum vinegar.

Keep pickles always in a cool place.

Small cucumbers called gherkins are pickled in the same way except that steaming is not necessary. Omit the onions and add to the last vinegar a tablespoonful of sugar.

The bag of spices may be removed when the pickles are flavored sufficiently.

TARRAGON VINEGAR FOR SALADS.

Put a bunch of tarragon leaves in one quart of fine cider vinegar in an earthen vessel set within another containing cold water. Set on the fire and let the vinegar boil up.

When cool, bottle and cork.

Only a small quantity of the tarragon should be used, as its flavor is very pronounced.

BAKED RHUBARB.

Put three cupfuls of skinned and cut-up rhubarb (or pie-plant) into an earthen dish; add one cupful of sugar; dredge with a teaspoonful of flour and bake (covered) about half an hour.

To be eaten with meats, or put into tart shells for dessert. Have covers for the tart shells.

HELPFUL SUGGESTIONS.

Salt toughens meat if added before it is done.

Wash lettuce carefully so as not to bruise, cutting each leaf from the stalk, and put it, dripping, into a closely covered pot. Set in a cool place. Lettuce thus prepared will keep for several days and be crisp and fresh.

Celery should be treated in the same way.

Each day look it over, rinse in fresh cold water and return to the pot.

Do not soak in water to freshen, but when slightly wilted, wash and put in an earthen pot instead.

Turnips, cabbage, and parsley are always improved by this treatment, but it is not necessary to pull the cabbage apart.

Greens, (spinach and sprouts) should be soaked for several hours in cold water.

Set asparagus bunches in a few inches of cold water to keep them fresh; the water should not come more than half way up the stalks. When ready to cook, wash in several waters to get out the sand.

Confectioner's sugar may be found at almost all shops where groceries are found, but when not procurable, powdered sugar will answer almost as well if it is rolled very fine on the moulding-board.

Make Coffee Bavarian Cream frequently, at least twice in a month. It is something one rarely tires of. When used as a dinner dessert, oranges served after it will be found very acceptable.

Candied fruits for pies or puddings may be softened by steaming in a steamer; set the fruit on a dish.

When wishing to keep a steak or chops over night in hot weather, if there is danger of spoiling, broil or fry over a hot fire just enough to sear the outside, and to heat through but not to cook. Set on ice.

If not cooked too much they will be as nice when broiled next morning as if they had not had the preliminary broil.

When cheese becomes too hard for the table, grate it and put away in bottles; it is useful for macaroni, soups, or sandwiches.

Empty all canned things, as soon as they are opened, into an earthen bowl, and if not used for a day or two, scald them. In this way tomatoes may be kept a week in a cool place.

Before putting crackers on the table set them in a hot oven a few minutes to crisp them.

Before toasting bread, dry it a little in the oven: it should be heated through before toasting. Serve dipped and buttered toast (on a separate dish) with fried salt pork or ham, at breakfast.

A little curry powder added to soups or stews gives a new dish.

When a quick fire is needed and the range burns slowly, rake out as thoroughly as possible; add a bundle of kindling-wood, and open the draughts. One bundle of wood is usually enough to bake a pan of biscuits or muffins. If the fire is to be used for broiling, burn the wood to a red bed of coals.

When broiling, if the fire is too hot, sprinkle over it a thin layer of fine ashes, or a handful of salt, or lay a folded sheet of newspaper on the coals; put on the lid, and when the paper has burned out, its ashes will smother the fire enough.

On the other hand, if the fire should not be hot enough, add a few scraps of fat meat.

Grape preserves may be put between layer-cake just before serving. For a small family, cut one layer crosswise (not to split) and double one half over the other. Served with cream, this makes a delicious dessert.

To brown flour for soups and gravies, put a few spoonfuls evenly on the bottom of a baking-pan and stir until it has become a fine amber-brown over a moderate fire. Bottle and keep for use.

Some different varieties of cheese are—Stilton, Camembert, Roquefort, New Roquefort, Brie, Gorgonzola, Club-House, Edam, Sweet Clover, Meadow Brook, Philadelphia Cream, Neufchatel, Parmesan, Old English, Limburger, Cheshire, Gruyère, and Pineapple.

An agreeable blend of tea is made of half a pound of the finest Oolong mixed with an ounce, or even less, of uncolored Japan tea. It (Japan) is of a pale greenish hue, and is not to be mistaken for the green tea of China.

Until one has become acquainted with the different grades and qualities of grocer's wares, it is much safer to buy only from houses whose judgment in such things can be depended on.

Dry egg-shells, break into bits, and put them away in a preserving jar to use in clearing coffee; two tablespoonfuls will clear one pint of coffee.

When dried chipped beef is in danger of becoming musty, take it from the box, spread on a platter and dry it in a hot oven; it may then be put away and will keep for months. When immersed in cream sauce, beef treated in this way will swell to its natural size and be as nice as at first.

Dried or smoked beef is considered by some physicians to be unsafe for food until cooked.

The chopping-bowl must be scraped and scoured after each using, and well scalded, otherwise it will become unhygienic. Turn upside-down when not in use.

Butter should be kept covered in a stone jar in a cool place; some housekeepers put it into a brine, and this certainly keeps it sweet, and sometimes improves the quality. The brine should be strong enough to bear up a potato.

Put a potato in the jar; add water, and then stir in salt until the potato floats.

Get only the best and sweetest butter, and never use an inferior grade for cooking.

Rancid butter is unhealthful.

As soon as possible after it comes from the butcher's hands, remove meat from the paper, put it on an earthen dish and set in a cool place.

Spread out in a thin layer berries of every sort, and keep them in a cool, dry, and dark place. If they seem soft and not likely to keep, stew them in a sugar syrup.

Agate-ware pots with close-fitting covers make excellent cake-boxes.

Lettuce may be pulled apart, rinsed, and put directly on the ice in very hot weather, and be all the better for this treatment.

If meat is put on the ice, place between the ice and plate a thickness of flannel; this will keep the ice from melting too fast.

Cover the meat with a plate.

The refrigerator should be washed out thoroughly once a week with water in which a teaspoonful of sal-soda has been dissolved.

By keeping dishes containing food closely covered as much as possible, the refrigerator may be kept free from odors.

Baked onions are almost as delicious as those roasted in the ashes, or before the logs in the open fireplace.

Do not peel them, but set them in a hot oven to bake until tender. Take off the skins carefully and serve with butter, salt, and pepper.

"China eggs" are a pretty garnish to a dish of hashed meat or picked-up fish; boil them just hard enough to make them shell easily, and serve whole and hot.

Let cake cool a little before taking it from the pans.

When testing cake to see if it is baked enough, use a slender broom-straw, thrusting it gently into the edge first, and then into the middle; if put into the middle part suddenly, or too soon, the cake may fall.

Before scraps of bread have a chance to become musty, dry them thoroughly in the oven; put away in a covered jar, and when enough has accumulated, roll to powder on the moulding board, and put into jars or tin boxes for breading, etc.

Scraps of Neufchatel or cream cheese may be made to serve again by mixing them with butter and cream, or milk, and spreading them on banquet crackers. Make into sandwiches and serve with salad.

FLAVORINGS.

Vanilla, almond, rose, coffee, caramel, maraschino, chopped almonds, grated cocoanut, pounded macaroons, fruit juices, rum, pistachio, orange, lemon, kirsch, sherry, brandy, madeira, curacoa, chocolate, orange-flower water, cordials, and liqueurs form most of the flavorings in general use.

Mrs. Sherwood gives the following rules for the service of wine at a dinner party:

White wine with the fish, sherry with the soup, and claret and champagne with the roast; champagne is either "dry" or sweet, and must not be decanted, but must be kept in ice-pails and opened when needed.

Catering for Two. 269

Madeira and port wines accompany the game; these are decanted, and should not be cold, but of the temperature of the room.

A delicious claret-punch for luncheons or suppers is made from claret, vichy, lemons, sugar, and cracked ice, in proportions to suit the taste.

Sherbets and sorbets are served in glasses after the game.

Roman-punch is a lemon sherbet to which Jamaica rum has been added in the proportion of one cupful of rum to one quart of sherbet.

For a lemon sherbet, boil together for twenty minutes, one pint of sugar, and one scant quart of water, and when cool, add a cupful of lemon-juice and the grated rind of two lemons; mix together and freeze until firm.

Strawberry and orange sherbets are made in the same way, adding a little lemon-juice. A mixture of fruit juices makes delicious sherbets or sorbets; the latter are sherbets only half frozen.

A portion of the dinner-roll dough may have stoned dates worked into it; this is called date bread and is delicious for luncheon. Put the dates in close together, and let it raise the same as any bread dough. To be eaten cold.

Potatoes should be thinly pared, as the best part lies next the skin.

The sweetness of fruit also lies next the skin.

Never throw away milk or cream because it has soured: allow it to become loppered, or thick, and use it for corn-bread or griddle-cakes. When thick and ice cold, it may be whipped with the egg-beater and it makes then a refreshing drink in hot weather. Whip it about five minutes. Sour milk and molasses both contain lactic acid, an element found in gastric juice. Lactic acid is a digestive ferment.

Soured (unsweetened) condensed milk may have two parts or a little more of water added to it, when it may be used in cooking the same as other sour milk.

Eggs must be cold and very fresh to whip well.

When the white of an egg after being frothed begins to separate, a few drops of lemon-juice added will remedy the trouble.

Always use earthen-ware for whisking eggs in.

Nasturtiums make a pretty as well as an appetizing garnish for meats and salads; to be at their best they must be freshly picked. The stems as well as the blossoms are edible.

Florists now sell them in pots so that they are easily obtainable for use on the table.

In serving fresh peaches peel, stone, and

halve. Do not slice, but serve in halves, with a lump of ice in each, with sugar to taste.

After peeling, cover with a wet cloth; set on ice until well chilled, and add ice and sugar at serving-time.

In canning fruits, turn the filled jars upside-down for a week, examining them each morning.

If any juice exudes, the jar is not air-tight, and the contents are likely to spoil: such must be cooked over again, or be used very soon.

To blanch is to scald with boiling water so that skins of fruits, nuts, or sweetbreads, etc., may be removed with greater ease.

A nice filling for sandwiches may be made by mincing or pounding meat very fine, mixing it to a paste with cream or melted butter, and seasoning to taste.

THINGS TO KEEP ON HAND.

Canned tomatoes, corn, milk, sardines, salmon, potted ham, salt pork, flour, soda, baking-powder, salt, sugar, eggs, macaroni, butter, cheese, molasses, spices, vinegar, crackers, tea, coffee, cocoa, chocolate, smoked-beef, lemons, pepper, mustard, Indian-meal, hominy, corn-starch, oat-meal, potatoes, apples, cabbage or celery, onions, olives, capers, extract of beef, salt codfish, rice, tapioca, lima-beans, fruit cake, maple-sugar, and honey : also soap, starch, blueing, borax, and sapolio.

Serve soufflés in separate courses ; omelettes also. Small sandwiches, or bread and cheese, may be passed with them.

A fish soufflé will take the place of a fish course.

The sweet Spanish peppers should be eaten with salt the same as radishes.

A continual change in the bill of fare is desirable : one tires of the same dessert if seen too often, no matter how delicious it is, unless possibly ice-cream may be an exception.

If part of a dish be left over, wait a day or two before serving it again, and let weeks elapse before preparing it again. In this way the table will always present a pleasant surprise.

Three tablespoonfuls of rice may be substituted for tapioca in the "tapioca méringue pudding."

Soak the rice over night in cold water, and add milk, eggs, etc., in the morning.

The little salt bags (ten-cent size) make roomy mittens for sweeping ; they will also be found of service about the stove, especially when removing dishes from hot ovens, as they protect both wrists and hands which a holder often fails to do.

Straining-cloths, dish-cloths, etc., should be thoroughly cleaned by boiling in washing soda or pearline; one teaspoonful to a quart of cold water.

In hot weather this should be done daily.

Rubber gloves protect the hands from vegetable and fruit stains; they are especially needed in making grape jelly.

Get them several sizes too large or the hand will not have room for free action.

Grease will melt them.

When a dish seems rather tasteless a dash of salt will often improve it. This also applies to pudding and other sweet dishes.

Jellies give zest to meats and vegetables, as do pickles also.

Olives, celery, and salted nuts are passed between the courses to prepare the palate for the dishes which are to follow.

In cooking vegetables, those of one size should be selected, if possible, otherwise the larger ones should be cut into pieces to equal the smaller.

Onions may be cut nearly through, leaving just enough uncut to hold the pieces together. In this way all will be cooked at the same time.

The earthen pipkin is a valuable cooking

utensil, as it may be easily kept sweet and clean, and things cook evenly and keep hot in it.

A "cupful" in all cases is half a pint.

Any preserved citron which is left over at springtime may be drained from the syrup, dried a little in the oven and packed away in glass to be used in cakes and puddings at any time: thus prepared it will keep for years.

Pork tenderloins may be cut in three-quarter-inch slices (across instead of lengthwise) breaded with cracker crumbs and fried the same as directed for veal cutlets; serve with lemon marmalade, or apple jelly and pickled tomatoes, or they may be broiled.

Left-over stewed potatoes may be mashed fine with a fork, minced parsley added, formed into cakes, dipped into cracker crumbs and fried delicately in a little butter; they are delicious prepared in this way.

Left-over mashed potatoes are excellent breaded with cracker crumbs, fried in butter and used as a border around hashed meats; lay a sprig of parsley or watercress on each cake.

Keep a bottle of linseed-oil and lime-water (mixed in equal parts) in readiness to use for burns or scalds. Shake well, spread upon old table-linen, and bind on the injured place.

TO DRAW POULTRY.

Make an incision in the breast end of the turkey, take out the crop, loosen the windpipe and the other long stringy tube, cutting them out as low down as possible, which will make the drawing of the lower entrails easier.

Cut a slit across the lower end of the fowl between leg and tail large enough to admit the hand. Slip in the hand straight, pressing the back of the hand close to the side of the body and between body and entrails; push up as far as possible; now curve the fingers, catch the entrails at the upper end, and draw out the entire mass, slowly, so as not to break the gall, which is a little green sac lying against the liver, and which if crushed will give a bitter taste to everything it touches.

Take out the liver and heart; cut off any green portion on the liver where the gall has rested; wash quickly and put away.

Cut the gizzard open; tear out the lining; wash and scrape it thoroughly and put it away.

Cut out all pieces of nice fat found among the entrails, and after washing lay it over the turkey to keep it moist when roasting.

Cut out the oil-sac on the tail.

Always buy fat poultry: there is no economy in thin, scrawny meat of any kind, especially poultry.

COOKING UTENSILS.

Wire spoon, cooking spoons, knives and forks, can-opener, apple-corer, iron dish-cloth, flour-sifter, sugar-scoops, quart, pint, half-pint and gill measures, one iron spider, two small sheet-iron frying-pans, one large sheet-iron frying-pan, half a dozen saucepans of assorted sizes, earthenware pudding-dishes, bread and cake tins, one large pot over which a steamer will fit, two dripping-pans for roasting, one to fit over the other, wire broiler, graters, coffee-grinder, close-fitting covers for all pots, pans, etc., chopping-bowl and -knife, potato-masher, wooden pestle, flour-dredge, moulding-board, rolling-pin, teakettle, canisters for tea, coffee, and spices, Universal pot, pipkins — several sizes, bread pot, small knife for paring vegetables, whetstone, muffin rings, gem or muffin pans, pie plates, biscuit tins, meat-racks, tea-stands, coffee-strainer, sieves, meat-grinder, long clinch-nails for skewers, skimmer, cake-turner, wooden spoons, colanders, saw bread-knife, yellow earthen bowls, meat-block, two funnels ; one small for bottles, a large one for jugs.

TO LAY THE DINNER-TABLE.

The table should first be covered with a cloth of thick cotton flannel which comes for this purpose, securely fastened on by pinning the corners together underneath.

Over this spread the damask cloth.

A circular mirror or a piece of embroidered linen may fill the centre of the table for the flowers to stand on. At the right of each place put a dessert-spoon, teaspoon, a knife for the salad course, a larger knife for the meat course, soup-spoon and oyster-fork, if oysters are served.

At the left, place two forks: if a fish course forms part of the meal add also a small fish-knife and -fork.

As each knife and fork is used it is removed with the plate, and the confusion and extra work of bringing in fresh knives and forks is avoided.

As the meal progresses, the table is gradually cleared, until, when the time for dessert arrives, nothing is left but the glasses, flowers, and the spoons for dessert. The space between the knives and forks should be wide enough for the dinner-plate, before which stands the salt-cellar, pepper-box, butter-plate, and glasses for water, Apollinaris, and wine.

Use tumblers for the ice-water, small tall glasses for Apollinaris, and appropriate glasses for the wine.

The napkin may hold the dinner-roll, or piece of bread, or the roll may be laid upon the butter-plate, which may also contain a pat of butter. All these arrangements make the serving of a dinner easier.

The bread, butter, and water should be put upon the table just before the meal is announced. The first course should be upon the table on sitting down, and the meat and vegetables in hot covered dishes be within easy reach on a side table. The salad may also be on the side table to replace the meat course as soon as it is removed.

Before serving the dessert, brush off all crumbs, then bring on coffee and fruit and the finger-bowls on the plates intended for fruit or bon-bons.

Olives, celery, salted nuts, pickles, or jellies should be on the table from the beginning of the meal: the first three are eaten between the courses; the pickles and jellies with the meat.

When there is no maid to wait at table, the side table is indispensable to the housewife who would save herself unnecessary steps, and have the dinner pass off without confusion.

The most convenient side tables are those in the form of an open closet, having a set of shelves, with large castors which render them easy to push about.

A table of this sort should contain all the extra knives, forks, and spoons, and other things needed for the meal, and, when possible, the food for the succeeding courses.

The lamp or gas-stove for hot water may also find a place here, and the dishes as they are removed from the dinner-table.

Griddle-cakes may be served from the side table, baked on the gas or oil stove; if the table is too high to permit of turning the cakes easily, put the stove on a waiter and set this on a chair.

Use a soapstone griddle, or wash thoroughly an old iron griddle, rub it with salt, and do not grease; the butter in the batter will be sufficient to keep cakes from sticking.

Let the table-linen be as fine and good as the purse will allow, and whenever possible have a few flowers on the table as a centrepiece.

A growing plant is in good taste, and the pot may be covered with green crèpe paper.

If the napery is not very fine, have it ironed very wet, with a heavy, hot iron until perfectly dry.

Water starch (that is extremely thin starch) may be used for the cloth but not for the napkins: thus treated, table linen will have a rich gloss and look well even if the quality is not the best and finest.

Colored cloths are out of place on the dinner table.

Colored napkins are used when the fruit comes on.

Doilies of drawn work at each place save the cloth, and serve to make the table attractive.

With linen perfectly laundered and spotless, glass sparkling, and the silver shining, a table may be elegant no matter how inexpensive the furnishings.

However informal the breakfast and luncheon, it is always well to make the dinner a meal of some ceremony.

Even if the viands are of the simplest, and the table appointments the plainest, a dinner served with regularity yields enjoyment and comfort to those partaking of it, and will be found to be less trouble than if served haphazard.

The style of putting all the dishes on the table at once is steadily growing out of favor in most families; it is found to be more conducive to the healthful enjoyment of food to serve but a few things at a time, making separate courses of the dishes whenever practicable. This plan tempts the appetite when too bountiful a supply of food would discourage it.

If only a very simple meal is desired (of two courses) add an extra vegetable, or increase the quantity of those mentioned, and select a somewhat rich dessert.

INDEX.

SOUPS.

Asparagus, cream of	108
Beans, purée of	136
Beef-tea	212
Bouillon (or consommé)	41
Celery soup	76
Chicken broth	7
Clam soup	143
Corn soup	163
Julienne consommé	98
Lamb broth, spiced	130
with lemon	48
Macaroni soup	56
Mutton broth	14
Ox-tail soup	87
Oyster stew	120
Peas, consommé with green	156
purée of green	62
Potato purée	35
Rice, consommé with	1
Soup with egg	27
Soup-stock (clear)	28
Split-pea soup	70
Tomato, bisque	20
cream purée	83
Vegetable soup	114

FISH.

Clam, chowder	140
fritters	221
Codfish, balls	204
picked-up	202
Fresh fish, boiled with Hollandaise sauce	93
broiled	209
fried	203
spiced	221
stuffed and baked	98
Oyster, cocktails	184
croustade	189
patties	194
pie	2
Oysters, escalloped	38
fried	106
on the half-shell	190
Salmon with Hollandaise sauce	195
Smelts, fried	190
Soufflé	195

MEATS.

Beef, à la mode	94
corned	23
frizzled	196
roast, porter-house	21
roast, sirloin	8
soup-meat	42
steak, Hamburg	195
steak, porter-house	169
steak pudding	115
steak, round	6
steak with onions	144
stew (cold roast)	23
stew with sweet potatoes	13
tongue	192
various ways of using the coarse ends	171

Birds	222
Chicken, blanquette of	190
broiled	168
browned in butter	57
croquettes (of birds)	222
fricassee	44
fried	57
patties	194
roast	43
smothered	201
soufflé	194
Duck, roast	152
Hash	23
baked	213
Lamb, browned in spiced sauce	129
chops, breaded (French)	185
broiled	77
cutlets and stew from roast	50
roast	29
stuffed	49
stew	30
Liver and bacon	208
Meat pie, baked	67, 72
Mutton, boiled, caper sauce	15
Pork.	
bacon and eggs	208
ham, baked (smoked)	157
fried, cream gravy (smoked)	36
omelette	207
on toast	210
roast, savory stuffing (fresh)	148
pork and beans	121
chops, fried, cream gravy	84
roast rib and loin	125
tenderloin, fried and boiled	84, 274
sausage, fried and baked	204
meat	225
souse (pickled pigs' feet)	224

Pot-roast, mutton	39
stew with lamb kidneys	165
top-sirloin	71
under-round or cross-rib	164
Potted meats	220
Remnants, of cold oven roasts or broils, 126,	197
poultry, veal, or lamb	197
Turkey, roast	175
Veal, cutlets	109
loaf	210
pot-pie (raised crust)	63
roast (stuffed)	88

VEGETABLES.

Asparagus on toast	91
Beans, butter	101
lima	59
string	101
Beets	137
Cabbage, fried	158
hot slaw	100
Cape May omelette	52
Cauliflower, fritters	64
with Hollandaise sauce	166
Corn, on the cob	66
fritters	234
stewed	36
Cucumbers	101
with cream	221
Greens (beet-tops, dandelions, and spinach)	111
Hominy, boiled	126
fried	36
Macaroni with cheese	9
Onions, baked in milk	138
boiled	90
browned in butter	131
roasted in the oven	267

Parsnip, buttered	45
patties	37
with cream sauce	16
Peas, green (stewed)	52
Potatoes, baked	79
balls (baked)	153
boiled (new)	212
with cream sauce	51
breaded	213
broiled	165
browned in milk	110
in the oven	117
cakes	99, 274
croquettes	137
escalloped	31
fried	165
French	95
hashed, or stewed, with cream gravy	158
with parsley	59
lyonnaise	9
mashed	73
Saratoga chips	130
sweet, baked or broiled	150
browned in the oven	85, 150
Rice, boiled	16
croquettes	89
fried	44
Spaghetti with tomato sauce	227
Spinach with egg sauce	111
Squash, baked	145
mashed	90
Succotash	95
Tomatoes, baked	65
escalloped	45
fritters	225
on toast	74
stewed	117
in butter	37

Turnips and potatoes mashed together 24, 145
    breaded 149
    browned in butter 86
    with cream sauce 31

SALADS.

Salad, apple 95
    asparagus 139
    cabbage 53
    celery 24
    chicken 102
    chicory, with French dressing . . 32
    cold meat 141
    cold slaw 38
    egg, with greens 112
    lettuce, with French dressing . . 60
    onion 117
    oyster 45
    potato, with greens 131
        for tea or luncheon . . . 200
    sardine 214
    string-bean 160
    sweetbread 200
    tomato 9, 112
        and celery 191

DESSERTS.

Apples, baked, with cream . . . 161
    with méringue 155
Cake.
    cake, chocolate 113
        cream 113
        fruit 236
        gold and silver 236
        lemon 10, 11
        loaf 53

Cake—(Continued)
- molasses 237
- pound 237
- sponge 226
- whipped-cream 10
- chocolate custard for layer cake . . 223
- frosting for cakes and puddings . 11, 232
- gingersnaps 238
- hot ginger bread and wafers . . . 239
- soft gingerbread 240
- vanilla wafers 119

Charlotte russe 173
Custard, boiled 154
Dumplings, steamed, caramel sauce . . 17
Floating island 118
French toast 235
Fruit dumplings, baked . . . 81
  fritters 234
Gelatine jelly, caramel 5
  caramel sea-foam moussê . . 230
  chocolate, with custard . . . 154
  coffee, Bavarian cream . . . 229
  orange, with whipped cream . . 178
  pineapple, with whipped cream . . 60
  princess, with sea-foam cream . . 151
  strawberry 68
    whip 229
  wine 91
Ice-cream 185
Muskmelon with ice-cream and fruit . 234
Pie, apple 104
  cherry 105
  huckleberry 167
  lemon méringue 39
  mince 181
  peach 104
  rhubarb 104
  squash 166

Pineapple, jardinière 182
  with floating island 152
Pudding, banana méringue . . . 168
  blackberry 141
  cherry 40
  chocolate 139
    jelly, with sea-foam cream . . 127
  corn-starch, with candied fruit . . 25
    lemon méringue (baked) . . 153
  cottage 112
  farina 6
  Indian 123
  lemon méringue 66
  orange tapioca, with whipped cream . 32
  plum 178
  prune 96
  queen's 173
  rice, baked 160
    boiled, whipped-egg sauce . . 232
    méringue 272
  roly-poly, with whipped-egg sauce . 3
  steamed, with oranges . . . 146
  suet 107
  sultana 161
  tapioca, baked 75
    cream 134
    méringue 86
Strawberry shortcake 46

SAUCES.

MEAT AND VEGETABLE SAUCES.

Cream gravy, for bacon, etc. . . . 209
  for fresh pork 84
Onion butter 199
Sauce, bread 223
  caper 15
  curry 199

Sauce—*(Continued)*
  drawn butter (or white) . . . 16, 90
  Espagnole (or brown), for stews, etc. . 198
  Hollandaise 94
  mint 51
  parsley 51
  tartare 190
  wine 51

PUDDING SAUCES.

Caramel (burnt sugar) 18
Maple-sugar syrup 202
Sauce, caramel 18
  caramel cream 189
  custard 47
  egg, whipped 4
  hard 82, 180
  liquid 107, 180
  strawberry-shortcake 233
  tutti-frutti 233
  wine 180
Sea-foam cream 232
Substitute for whipped cream . . . 34
Sugar syrup 234
Whipped cream 33

SALAD DRESSINGS.

French dressing 24, 32
Mayonnaise 46, 103, 141
Tarragon vinegar 261

TABLE-SAUCES.

Apples, fried 158
Apple-sauce, baked 127
  hot 85

Cranberry-sauce, strained 177
   whole 178
Peaches, stewed and baked . . . 12
Prunes, stewed 12
Rhubarb, baked 261
   stewed 88
Strawberries, raspberries, and blackberries, stewed 11

PICKLES AND RELISHES.

Chili sauce 150
Marmalade, lemon 79
   tomato 138
Pickled, cabbage 4
   cucumbers 260
   green tomatoes 259
   string-beans 260
Spiced tomato sauce, cold . . . 172
   hot 122

JELLIES.

Jelly, crab-apple 254
   currant 256
   grape 255
   quince 250

PRESERVES.

Canned, cherries 251
   peaches 247
   plums 251
   strawberries, raspberries, and blackberries 11
Preserved, citron 253
   grapes 252
   orange-peel (candied) 247

Preserved, peaches	248
spiced	249
pineapple	250
candied	105
quinces	250
Syrup from berries	257

BREAD

Biscuits (baking-powder)	159
or dinner rolls (yeast)	132
Bread (yeast)	133
date (yeast)	269
gluten (yeast)	218
milk (yeast)	215
Cornbread	123, 226
Muffins (baking-powder)	206
Graham	213
Indian meal	224
yeast (prune pudding batter)	97

MISCELLANEOUS.

Bread-crumbs for breading and puddings	212
Cheese, on toast	203
some varieties	265
Chocolate	162
Coffee	147, 245
Cooking utensils	276
Crust, for oyster-patties	193
for pot-pies and stew-pies	159
Eggs, au gratin	192
beauregarde	188
poached	206
scrambled	207
Flavorings	268
Fondant, or foundation, for cream candies	241
Frosting for cakes and puddings	11, 232

Index.

Grape-fruit	188
Griddle-cakes, bread	211
buckwheat	214
wheat and Indian	211
Helpful suggestions	262
Home-made yeast	219
Indian-meal mush	205
Lemonade	258
Lemon extract	258
Milk toast	202
Mince-meat	181, 246
Oatmeal	205
Oranges	19
Pie-crust (flaky)	103
Pot-cheese with watercresses	81
Punch	269
Salted almonds	80
Sandwiches	271
cheese	32, 268
sardine	214
Sherbets and sorbets	269
Stuffing, bread and butter	49, 126
onion	152
Sugar-plums, chocolate cream-bar, and nut candies	242
Tea	26
Things to keep on hand	271
To draw poultry	275
To lay the dinner-table	276
Unfermented grape-juice	257
Vanilla extract	258

www.ingramcontent.com/pod-product-compliance
Lightning Source LLC
Chambersburg PA
CBHW032042230426
43672CB00009B/1442